AT-RISK,
LOW-ACHIEVING STUDENTS
IN THE CLASSROOM

The Authors

Judy Brown Lehr, an Assistant Professor of Education at Furman University, Greenville, South Carolina, teaches at both the graduate and undergraduate level. She also directs the Center of Excellence Project, a special grant to train teachers to teach at-risk, low-achieving students.

Hazel Wiggins Harris is Professor of Education, Associate Dean for Summer Sessions, and Director of Graduate Studies at Furman University, Greenville, South Carolina.

The Advisory Panel

David Bell, Director of Teacher Education Services, Henderson State University, Arkadelphia, Arkansas

Mary M. Daniel, second grade teacher, Gateway Elementary School, Travelers Rest, South Carolina

Dana T. Elmore, Professor, Teacher Education Division, San Jose State University, California

Terry Gillespie, Science teacher, Rich High School, Park Forest, Illinois

Cynthia E. Glass, Reading Specialist, Wilson Middle School, Natick, Massachusetts

Steve Hoppin, School Psychologist, Jefferson County, Colorado

Jannelle Martin, Mathematics teacher, Travelers Rest High School, South Carolina

Evelyn J. Mims, Teacher of English-Speech/Drama, Central High School, Tuscaloosa, Alabama

Sallie Hickok Spiller, Elementary Guidance Counselor, Roanoke County Schools, Virginia

Cynthia Thomas-Hardwick, Reading Specialist and Teacher of the Learning Disabled, Wintersville High School, Ohio

Thelma Thompson, Principal, M. S. Bailey Elementary School, Clinton, South Carolina

Patricia VanAntwerp, fourth grade teacher, North Watervliet Elementary School, Michigan

AT-RISK, LOW-ACHIEVING STUDENTS IN THE CLASSROOM

Judy Brown Lehr
Hazel Wiggins Harris

nea PROFESSIONAL LIBRARY
National Education Association
Washington, D.C.

ACKNOWLEDGMENT

The authors wish to thank the dedicated educators from the Center of Excellence Model Schools for their assistance in developing this publication:

School	*District*
Bakers Chapel Elementary School	School District of Greenville County
Belton Elementary School	Anderson District Two
Cannons Elementary School	Spartanburg District Three
Gateway Elementary School	School District of Greenville County
Hendrix Elementary School	Spartanburg District Two
Liberty Elementary School	Pickens County
M. S. Bailey Elementary School	Laurens District 56
Tamassee Elementary School	Oconee County

Printing History

First Printing:	July 1988
Second Printing:	April 1989
Third Printing:	January 1991
Fourth Printing:	June 1992
Fifth Printing:	June 1993

Note

The opinions expressed in this publication should not be construed as representing the policy or position of the National Education Association. Materials published by the NEA Professional Library are intended to be discussion documents for educators who are concerned with specialized interests of the profession.

Library of Congress Cataloging-in-Publication Data

Lehr, Judy Brown.
　At-risk, low-achieving students in the classroom.

　(Analysis and action series)
　Bibliography: p.
　1. Underachievers.　2. Slow learning children.
3. Remedial teaching.　4. Motivation in education.
I. Harris, Hazel Wiggins.　II. Title.　III. Series.
LC4661.L393　1988　371.92'6　88-15106
ISBN 0-8106-3338-8

CONTENTS

INTRODUCTION

Experts across the country are questioning the effects of the educational reform movement on certain groups of students. The assertion is made that many times low achievers have been ignored in the planning and intervention efforts; therefore the gap has widened between these students and their higher-achieving peers. Furthermore, demographic data shows growth in the at-risk population. More and more students are at risk of school failure. What are the reasons? Complicated economic and social forces may cause the problems. But the reality is that these hard-to-teach students exist in the schools—they are the ones who have unique needs and who require more and more of the classroom teacher.

This book is not intended to be a cookbook approach for teachers to use in the classroom because teaching is a multidimensional professional activity, not a technique. What we have tried to do is share ideas from classroom observation of teachers who have been particularly successful with at-risk students and suggest that other teachers implement the ideas that are appropriate for their own classrooms.

After reviewing the voluminous research in the field, we have emphasized its practical applications to classroom teachers because we believe the role of research is to guide practitioners. When some of these ideas were implemented by a local elementary school faculty in South Carolina in a one-year period, student test scores showed remarkable improvement (85).* For example, among fourth graders in 1986, 9 percent performed above and 26 percent below expectations in reading on the California Test of Basic Skills; in language, 16 percent were above, 11 percent below; and in arithmetic, 11 percent were above and 8 percent below.

---

*Numbers in parentheses appearing in the text refer to the Bibliography beginning on page 94.

But in the 1987 testing of these children as fifth graders, 27 percent scored above expectations in reading and only 2 percent below; in language, 38 percent were above, 1 percent below; and in arithmetic, 57 percent scored above and 1 percent below. All grades showed improvement but the fourth and fifth grades made the biggest gains (85)—almost eliminating low achievement.

We cannot promise readers this dramatic increase in test scores, nor do we mean to imply that tests measure success. But based on our experience, classroom teachers do get positive results when they emphasize developing the total child into a productive member of society.

Chapter 1

WHO IS THE AT-RISK LOW ACHIEVER?

CHARACTERISTICS

A review of the literature does not indicate a published definition of the at-risk, low-achieving student. Instead, the term *low achieving* encompasses many groups of students who have special characteristics or needs. Possible labels for these students include the following:

- disadvantaged
- culturally deprived
- underachiever
- nonachiever
- low ability
- slow learner
- less able
- low socioeconomic status
- language-impaired
- dropout-prone
- alienated
- marginal
- disenfranchised
- impoverished
- underprivileged
- low-performing
- remedial

Labels define clusters of attributes rather than sets of distinct and individual qualities, however. Can low achievers be labeled? Should they be labeled? If this group is labeled, will the students be treated differently? Hobbs warns that

> Categories and labels are powerful instruments for social regulation and control, and they often are employed for obscure, covert or hurtful purposes: to degrade people, to deny them access to opportunity, to exclude "undesirables" whose presence in society in some way offends, disturbs familiar customs, or demands extraordinary efforts. (67)

Research supports the belief that some teachers do communicate inappropriate expectations toward students they believe to be less capable. Students categorized by teachers as at-risk are treated differently from high achievers. For example, sometimes these students are (55, 53, 44, 56, 135)—

- seated farther away from the teacher.
- given less direct instruction.

9

- offered fewer opportunities to learn new material.
- asked to do less work.
- called on less often.
- given less wait time.
- questioned primarily at the knowledge/comprehension levels.
- not prompted when they do not know the answer to a question.
- given less praise.
- rewarded for inappropriate behavior.
- criticized more frequently.
- given less feedback.
- interrupted more often.
- given less eye contact and other nonverbal communication of attention and responsiveness.

Teachers' expectations about students' ability or inability to learn may sometimes become self-fulfilling prophecies. Not all of the above behaviors need to be exhibited to bring about self-fulfilling prophecies, however. If, for example, low-achieving students are assigned considerably less content than they can handle, that factor alone will reduce their learning (53).

But as Kerman points out, "The ways some teachers treat low-achieving students should not be construed as an indictment of teachers, since the biases demonstrated in teacher/student interactions are, in most cases, unconscious" (83). Alerting teachers to the unconscious behaviors they exhibit toward at-risk students is a first step toward change. Developing effective staff development programs like T.E.S.A. (Teacher Expectations and School Achievement) is another (83).

The focus of this monograph is not to emphasize the wrong ways of teaching low achievers. However, we think it is helpful to understand what actually happens to many of these students in the educational system. And it is important that professionals change unconscious behavior to more effective conscious behavior. Our thrust then, will be to use the research to look at ways administrators and teachers can avoid labeling and giving students unequal opportunities to learn.

This monograph defines the at-risk student as one who is not working up to potential. The term "at-risk" or "low-achieving" is relative. For example, at one time even Albert Einstein was labeled a low achiever. Certain characteristics are often present with low achievers, but none are absolute.

The following list contains characteristics we have identified as a result of our research and experience. All these traits need not be present for a student to be identified as at risk.

Possible Characteristics of the At-Risk, Low-Achieving Student

- Academic difficulties
- Lack of structure (disorganized)
- Inattentiveness
- Distractibility
- Short attention span
- Low self-esteem
- Health problems
- Excessive absenteeism
- Dependence
- Discipline problem
- Narrow range of interest
- Lack of social skills
- Inability to face pressure
- Fear of failure (feels threatened by learning)
- Lack of motivation

Low achievers have academic difficulties, but with altered teaching methods, many of them are able to learn. These students are often disorganized and need assistance in planning and goal-setting; they may be inattentive and easily distractible with short attention spans. Effective teachers use a variety of materials and strategies to keep their interest. Since many low achievers also have a negative self-image, supportive learning environments can help build more positive self-esteem. Health problems and excessive absenteeism can be other characteristics of these students.

At-risk students may be very dependent. They have not had enough successful experiences to enable them to rely on and trust their own abilities. They can be discipline problems unless an appropriate positive classroom management system is in place. The

11

narrow range of interest exhibited by some low achievers often can be related to their socioeconomic level. The curriculum of the home is an important consideration in helping them succeed (118, 119). Because some low achievers lack social skills, we advocate helping them acquire these skills by structuring the environment to facilitate more peer interaction. Finally, some low achievers are so afraid of failing that they will not even try. Effective teachers structure the learning tasks in small sequential steps. By experiencing success, at-risk students can be motivated to learn.

As Doyle observes,

> Many secondary school students, despite their ability, will not expend the effort to achieve their potential. Underachievement can become a way of life. Once students begin believing they have failed because they lack ability, they tend to lose hope for future success. They develop a pattern of academic hopelessness and stop trying. (41)

Attribution theory, a cognitive theory of motivation that deals with perceived causes of success and failure in achievement, has been used to explain why some students usually experience success while others seem doomed to fail. It holds that when students understand the relationship between achievement and effort, they can begin to feel in charge of their lives and responsible for their fate (71).

LEARNING STYLE

Remarkable scientific advances have been made recently in understanding the human brain. Researchers have verified that the two sides of the brain perform different functions; numerous technical books have been written about hemispheric specialization. These differences in brain function cause individual learning style differences (28). Nevertheless, much of today's education continues to be dominated by a left-brained curriculum—perhaps because textbooks are the mainstay of the classroom process (146, 117).

According to Carbo, Dunn, and Dunn, right-brained-preferenced students—

> are less bothered by sound when studying; in fact, they may like things that appear to be distractors to lefts—such as noise, people, movement or food while learning; often prefer dim illumination; usually re-

12

quire an informal design; are less motivated toward conventional schooling than lefts; are less persistent; prefer learning with peers, and prefer tactual more than either auditory or visual stimulation—even at the high school level. (28)

Research findings concerning environmental factors—sound, light, design, time of day, mobility, and temperature preferences—demonstrate the importance of complementing individuals' learning style preferences with the instructional environment. For example, "Environmental elements affect approximately 10% of the total school age population and underachievers are the students for whom the environment is most important" (28).

A review of the literature on cognitive style indicates considerable evidence that students from different ethnic groups learn differently. Cognitive style refers to individual preferences based on differences in cognition, personality, and perception. Researchers have concluded that the cognitive strategy of Black students, for example, differs from that required in the mainstream educational setting; this results in a conflict between teaching and learning styles (48). Other researchers such as Apple (4) and Young (162) describe how schools promote docility, minimal socialization, and competition. According to Frechtling, "These demands may clash with the socially interactive Black child, accustomed to greater stimulation. The results may be a bored and inattentive child, who sees school as relatively unstimulating, constraining and monotonous" (48).

Students who experience academic difficulties have learning styles that are extremely different from those of the gifted or highly achieving population. In reviewing the research in this area, Carbo, Dunn, and Dunn state that—

Initially, underachievers often require an informal design; they find it difficult to sit on wooden or steel chairs for more than a few minutes. Such children also appear to prefer learning either with classmates through small-group techniques or directly with their teacher; they lack the independent skills and ability to learn alone, and they do not derive much satisfaction from large group instruction where they must patiently wait their turn and consistently compete with classmates. Underachievers usually find it difficult to learn by listening; the ability to remember what they have heard seems to be their most difficult task. Neither are they strong visual learners; but they do achieve well when involved kinesthetically and tactually. Such children learn most easily through a multi-sensory approach that introduces new material through their strongest perceptual modality and reinforces through their secondary and then tertiary strength. (28)

In examining the characteristics of low-achieving students, educators agree that these students process information differently—in ways that in many cases are in direct opposition to the ways in which present classrooms are structured. Rather than dwelling on the negative characteristics of at-risk students, however, it might be well to ask why these students are not grasping the material. There is a big difference between looking at the student as the problem and labeling the student, and looking at the system as the problem and finding ways to improve the system. In an attempt to improve the system, the remainder of this book offers suggestions and strategies to help teachers help low achievers become successful learners.

Chapter 2

ORGANIZING THE LEARNING ENVIRONMENT FOR LOW ACHIEVERS

Low achievers are often at risk of becoming dropouts, mentally and physically. To encourage these students to remain in school, the learning environment must be organized for them to succeed. Studies indicate that many programs designed to reduce the number of school dropouts do not give serious attention to changing teacher and administrator attitudes toward these students or to methods of teaching them (116). This chapter focuses on the essentials of a learning environment in which at-risk students can succeed and on the roles of the principal, the teacher, and the parents in achieving this goal.

EFFECTIVE SCHOOLS RESEARCH

How Many Do You Need To See?

How many effective schools would you have to see to be persuaded of the educability of all children? If your answer is more than one, then I submit that you have reasons of your own for preferring to believe that basic pupil performance derives from family background instead of school response to family background. Whether or not we will ever effectively teach the children of the poor is probably far more a matter of politics than of social science and that is as it should be.

We can, whenever and wherever we choose, successfully teach all children whose schooling is of interest to us. We already know more than we need to do that. Whether or not we do it must finally depend on how we feel about the fact that we haven't so far. (42)

One of the most important achievements of educational research in the last 20 years has been the identification of effective schools, especially those that are successful in teaching basic skills to children from low-income families (143, 17). The effective schools movement began when observant educators noticed that some schools were more effective than others in raising the achievement and morale of poor children and children of ethnic groups who could no longer be identified on the basis of test results (116, 42).

Effective schools have certain characteristics in common:

- vigorous instructional leadership
- a principal who makes clear, consistent, and fair decisions
- an emphasis on discipline and a safe and orderly environment
- instructional practices that emphasize basic skills and academic achievement
- collegiality among teachers in support of student achievement
- teachers with high expectations that all students can and will learn
- frequent review of student progress.

The literature on effective schools reveals very definite factors that increase the likelihood of success for all students, but especially for low achievers. In these schools principals, teachers, students, and parents agree on the goals, methods, and content of education (13, 34, 41, 47, 108, 141, 19, 42).

THE ROLE OF THE PRINCIPAL

The principal is a key element in determining success for at-risk students. Research suggests that teacher perceptions of the principal as an instructional leader are critical to the achievement of students, particularly low achievers (3). The successful principal creates an encouraging, supportive atmosphere for both students and teachers that enables them to take risks knowing that they will not be ridiculed if they are wrong but will be respected for trying.

A large body of scholarly research suggests that good school leaders protect the school day for teaching and learning. They reduce their teachers' administrative chores and classroom interruptions to a minimum. Effective principals build morale among their teachers. They develop community support for the school, its faculty, and its goals (108, 13, 116). To meet the needs of low-achieving students, schools must be reshaped into institutions that are less bureaucratic and more student focused (150). The school leader can provide this leadership by implementing the principles of Invitational Education.

Invitational Education

The literature on Invitational Education developed by William Purkey presents a framework for examining the influences of people, places, policies, programs, and processes on student success or failure. Purkey's book *Inviting School Success,* coauthored with John M. Novak (109) will be helpful to all educators who wish to create successful schools, especially schools that succeed with low achievers.

According to Purkey, "Invitational Education is the application of an emerging theory to practice and offers a defensible approach to the educative process and practical ways to make schools 'the most inviting place in town.'" (109). Specifically, invitational education is centered on four basic assumptions:

- People are able, valuable, capable of self-direction, and should be treated accordingly.
- The teaching/learning process is a cooperative alliance in which process is as important as product.
- People possess relatively untapped potential in all areas of human potential.
- This potential can best be realized by places, policies, programs, and processes that are intentionally designed to invite development and by people who consistently seek to realize this potential in themselves and others, personally and professionally.

When most faculty members are asked to describe their school on a checklist, only 15 to 35 percent ever describe their school or faculty as imaginative, adventurous, intellectually exciting, curious, initiating, playful—or even joyful. However, when asked to select the ten attributes most supportive of one's own growth, teachers always include adventurousness and intellectual excitement (63). Schools that implement invitational education create environments that invite adventure and joy in the workplace. They are caring places where people feel secure enough to take risks and grow personally and professionally.

Inviting Practices for Principals

School principals at the model schools for low-achieving students, which are a part of the Furman University Center of Excellence Project, have implemented many specific strategies based on the thesis of Invitational Education. Some of these techniques principals use with students and staff members follow.

With Students

Principal's "Pick of the Week"—Recognize students for academic and behavioral improvements.

Inviting Intercom—Begin and end each day on a positive note with a thought for the day.

Student Lunch Table—Have lunch with students, especially those who need a boost.

Extra Help—Set up a study hall and tutor students who need extra help.

Be a Cheerleader—Sponsor academic pep rallies and lead the first cheer.

Student/Teacher Sports Event—Encourage a faculty-student sports event. Often, low achievers can excel athletically.

Student Work Display—Encourage each teacher to display the work of *every* child in the classrooms and halls.

Names—Learn students' names and greet them personally.

Good Citizen—Ask each teacher to send one student to your office every day for a Good Citizen of the Day award.

Bus Ride—Show that you care by learning where your students live and joining them on the bus route.

Shadow—Select a low achiever and shadow him/her for the entire day. Then evaluate the student's instructional program.

With Staff Members

Professionalism—Treat all staff members as professionals. Show respect for their ideas and suggestions.

Make the Rounds—Each morning visit every classroom in the school. Carry a small note pad to record any staff concerns, schedule later appointments, etc.

Special Recognition—Draw the name of one staff member for employee of the month. Display the individual's picture and special personal information about her/him on a bulletin board.

Designate a reserved parking space for the employee of the month and/or the teacher of the year.

Model What You Expect—Be an active participant in all school-based staff development.

Be Caring—Remember staff birthdays, anniversaries, etc.

Teach for Your Teachers—Ask teachers to prepare a professional development plan and help them achieve it by teaching their classes.

Go with the Winners—The omnivores. Don't let a reticent faculty member diminish your enthusiasm.

Practice What You Preach—Say to teachers, "I won't ask you to do anything for students that I'm not willing to do for you."

Feedback—Put a suggestion box in the teachers' lounge and encourage the staff to give their ideas for school improvement.

Enhance Faculty Meetings—

- Have a drawing for door prizes–a new stapler, fast-food store coupons, a ream of paper.
- Show motivational films such as *Masters of Disaster*, *Cipher in the Snow*, *Johnny Lingo*.
- Encourage get-acquainted activities to help staff get to know each other on a personal level.
- Spotlight a grade level or subject area and have teachers share their successes.
- Serve refreshments—show that you care.

Promote Collegiality—Empower teachers to help make decisions: organize teams for budget and curriculum planning.

Have a Vision—Say no very carefully. Look for a way to make things happen.

Build Esprit de Corps—Encourage faculty members to participate in such activities as—

- Parties
- Breakfasts
- After-School Aerobics
- Sports Teams

Warm Fuzzies—Brag about the staff for perfect attendance, positive teaching practices, personal accomplishments, etc.

Incentive Plan—Develop a point system to reward accomplishments. Include such things as attendance, professional development, "golden trash can" (a cleanest room award determined by the custodian).

Maximum Payoff—Design staff development programs around teaching approaches with known potential for increasing student learning. Use peer coaching to implement the new strategy.

THE ROLE OF THE TEACHER

What is the role of the teacher in creating a learning environment that facilitates the achievement of the at-risk student? Chapter 4 presents the specific skills and competencies teachers need to succeed with low achievers based on the results of one successful project. This section reviews the available research on teacher effectiveness in creating a positive classroom environment for low achievers.

The literature supports the importance of the relationship between the teacher and the unsuccessful student. According to Ernest Boyer:

> Although we observed a variety of special programs for disadvantaged students, there was no single formula for success. However, at the heart of every effort that appeared to be succeeding, we noticed that there was a close relationship between a student and a counselor or teacher—there was a mentor with high standards and clear goals, one who had gained the student's confidence and trust. We recommend that programs be developed for high-risk students that provide special tutoring and a supportive relationship between a teacher and each student. (15)

The at-risk student has so often been labeled and put down that successful teachers are conscious of the need to develop this important bond. As Boyer continues, "In many cases these students have been alienated. Reversing this alienation begins with the establishment of a positive social bond between teachers and students" (15).

The following pages offer specific suggestions that teachers can use when working with low achievers in their classrooms. These

20

suggestions deal with teacher expectations, grouping, organization and planning, inviting practices, collegial learning, positive discipline, and cooperative learning.

Teacher Expectations

Successful teachers of low achievers have high expectations for all students. They believe that all can learn and that teachers must find the most effective way to teach them (1, 150, 109, 156, 56, 53). These teachers are persistent; they do not give up on students. Their attitude clearly communicates to the individual student that "You cannot get by in this class by passively sitting and playing dumb. You can learn and you will learn."

From a series of classroom observations Brophy and Good describe at least three types of teachers:

> *Proactive teachers* do not allow their expectations for low-achieving students to undermine their instructional activities. If anything, these teachers spend more time interacting with low-achieving students than with relatively high achievers. Furthermore, these teachers structure their classrooms and learning activities so that high-achieving pupils do not suffer because of the teachers' increased awareness of low-achieving students and the attention they direct toward them.
>
> The second group of teachers appears to be *reactive* in their classroom style. These teachers allow existing differences between high and low students to unfold so that high-achieving students, due to their own initiative and ability, come to dominate public classroom life. High-achieving students receive more response opportunities in such classrooms, but that is simply because they raise their hands more frequently and thus answer more questions.
>
> The third group of teachers is *overreactive.* They characteristically overemphasize student differences and supply qualitatively and quantitatively better treatment to high-achieving students than to low-achieving students. Such differences in teacher behavior exaggerate and extend initial differences between these two student groups. (56)

Underachievers, especially dependent, adult-oriented, and other-directed students, are particularly vulnerable to the possible effects of negative teacher expectations (72). This book assumes unquestionably that teachers want to be effective with low achievers. In many cases, however, they lack the necessary skills. With appropriate staff development, they can become proactive teachers with an attitude of self-efficacy.

21

Grouping

How should students be grouped—homogeneously or heterogeneously? Is tracking in high school recommended? Should students in General English have the same chance to take a class with a highly rated instructor as do those in American Literature? The best way to group students for instruction is a prevailing question. An extensive review of the literature on grouping practices in kindergarten through high school draws some frightening conclusions. A pattern of systematic discrimination against groups of lower-ability students warrants an examination. Murphy, Hallinger, and Lotto (100) use the phrase, opportunity to learn (OTL). They define it, as follows:

OTL = time + curriculum content covered + success rate + quality of instruction.

In the following list they show how the four aspects of OTL are distributed in an inequitable manner among instructional groups and curricular tracks:

TIME

For low-ability groups—
　　Instruction begins later in the class period
　　More instructional time lost during transitions
　　More time spent without a work assignment
　　More time lost due to student interruptions
　　More time lost due to teacher interruptions
　　Disproportionate amounts of instructional time spent in controlling and managing behavior
　　More class time devoted to homework
　　More off-task behavior
　　Instruction ends earlier in the period

INSTRUCTION

For low-ability groups–
　　Teachers feel less comfortable teaching
　　Teachers less knowledgeable about how to teach
　　Teachers spend less time preparing
　　Teachers hold lower performance expectations for self
　　Students are likely to receive instruction from aides
　　Negative and inappropriate performance expectations for students
　　Objectives less likely to be explained.

22

Materials introduced less clearly
Less time spent on introductory learning activities
Less interactive teaching; more worksheets
Less teacher clarity in presentations
More chaotic learning structure
Greater confusion as to appropriate modes of student participation
Fewer work standards provided
Students held less accountable for work
Reduced quality of teacher-student interactions
Less teacher enthusiasm and warmth

CURRICULUM CONTENT

For low-ability groups—
Content less academically oriented
Personal and social goals more important than academic objectives
Blurrred academic content
Lack of clear purpose and focus to classroom activities
Emphasis on therapy rather than learning
Fewer task-related interchanges between students and teachers
Material covered at slower pace
Lower-level objectives and functional skills emphasized
Fewer academic courses completed
Fewer academic standards specified
Fewer reports and projects assigned
Fewer homework assignments given
Less academic feedback provided
Fewer tests given
Little emphasis on skill progression
Less sequenced and integrated work in individual classes
More half-year courses
Fewer sequenced and integrated courses across years
Strong behavioral aspect to academic functions
Less counseling about appropriate course work to take

SUCCESS

In low-ability groups–
More off-task behavior
Less academic learning time
Lower rates of success

From "Inequitable Allocations of Alterable Learning Variables," by Joseph Murphy, Philip Hallinger, and Linda Lotto, *Journal of Teacher Education,* vol. 37, no. 6, November–December 1986. Copyright © 1986 by the American Association of Colleges for Teacher Education. Reprinted with permission.

The picture presented is widespread in our schools. According to Good and Brophy, "It is one evidenced by systematic and selective allocation of the favorable conditions of learning, systematic in that the distribution occurs in regular patterns and selective in that these resources are distributed in different fashions to the various instructional groups and curricular tracks" (56).

In his book *Tales Out of School*, Patrick Welsh, a teacher, paints a vivid picture of how the system discriminates against "tracked" students in a large suburban high school (151). Tracking, separating students into homogeneous groupings for high, average, and low achievers, "appears to be neither necessary, effective, nor appropriate"(23). Research suggests that all students, regardless of ability, can achieve at least as well in heterogeneous settings as in homogeneous settings. In fact, in three areas studied —access to knowledge, opportunities to learn, and classroom climate—tracking appears to lower the quality of education for both the average and the low-achieving student, and appears to promote negative expectations of performance. Thus, by tracking, schools may be sabotaging their own efforts to promote excellence and equality of education (103).

Even though many districts are seriously investigating grouping practices and attempting to make changes, the reality is that tracking does exist. Educators have used the following strategies to alleviate some of the negative effects of this kind of grouping:

- Rotating the instruction for each homogeneous group within the classroom to ensure that all groups have the chance to be the first group for instruction.

- Refusing to use watered-down texts with lower-tracked students.

- Using reading materials that relate to the lives and ethnic backgrounds of at-risk students.

- Varying teaching strategies but not subject matter.

- Rotating teachers within the building so that the most effective teachers have a low-track class as well as an advanced placement class.

- Requiring homework and having a set policy that makes students accountable if it is not completed. For example, students could complete homework during lunch or after school.

- Offering low achievers homework assistance such as a home-work hotline—a place to call for help. Some innovative school districts are offering homework assistance via local educational television stations.

- Implementing effective study skills programs for low-tracked students to teach them how to use a textbook, take notes, outline materials, and study for tests.

- Offering extra sessions after school to help at-risk students prepare for tests.

- Making students who fail accountable. Have a mandatory summer school program financed by the school district.

- Believing that lower-tracked students can learn and having high expectations for them. Push them to excel.

- Offering a summer "Think Camp" for teaching higher-level thinking skills to at-risk students. The CoRT program, developed by Edward deBono (38) has also been successful.

- Collaborating with a local university to develop a tutorial program for at-risk students.

- Implementing a summer program for at-risk students to work in local industries.

Organization and Planning

Effective teachers of low achievers are well organized. They know that the time students are actively engaged in learning contributes to their achievement. Time-on task research is particularly relevant to students working below their potential. Studies have shown that time spent directly on instruction is significantly related to achievement for disadvantaged children (21).

The Effective Use of Time program developed at the Peabody Center for Effective Teaching at Vanderbilt University is based on considerable research on the effective use of classroom time. When teachers are well organized and keep low-achieving students engaged in their tasks for longer periods of time, greater gains are made on reading achievement tests (67). Valuable time is wasted in classrooms where learners wait for the class to start, for the reading groups to gather, for papers to be passed out. In contrast, effective teachers use "sponge activities" to "sop up" waiting time otherwise lost (70). The following are several examples of sponge activities used by teachers in the elementary grades:

- List as many kinds of transportation as you can.
- List as many personal pronouns as you can.
- List as many countries in the world as you can.
- List as many animals as you can that begin with a vowel.

High school teachers have used these activities:

- List the presidential candidates for each party.
- List as many transitional words as you can.
- Make a list of women writers.

A problem written on the chalkboard for students to solve when they come to class can also be an effective sponge. For example:

If Magic Johnson is able to make three goals every minute, how many points will he have in a fifteen-minute period?

In efficient classrooms, both high- and low-achieving students work on their own, in study groups, and under the guidance of their teacher. According to one study, while high achievers were actively involved in learning for 70 percent of the time, students who were identified by their teachers as low achievers were actively involved only 50 percent of the time (21).

Teachers who plan also know the importance of attending to students' prior learning. As much as 80 percent of the variances in post-test scores may be accounted for by pre-test scores alone (12). Researchers have found, too, that about two-thirds of the variance in eleventh grade achievement could be predicted from third grade achievement (16). Unless low-scoring students receive instruction that builds on what they know and can do, then, they will probably remain low achievers. Teachers need to be well organized and find the correct place to begin instruction with these students. Successful teachers of low achievers, for example, use their planning time to analyze students' standardized test scores. Often they work in groups to try to determine exactly where the gaps are in student learning.

Inviting Practices for Teachers

Research is now providing ample evidence that when teachers better understand, accept, and like themselves, they have a much greater capacity to understand, accept, and like students (108). In a series of studies over a decade, Combs and associates investigated ways in which successful teachers organize their perceptions of themselves, others, and the world. Effective teachers may be clearly identified on the basis of their perceptions of people as able rather than unable, friendly rather than unfriendly, worthy rather than unworthy, dependable rather than undependable, helpful rather than hindering, and internally rather than externally motivated (109).

Though based on perceptual psychology, Invitational Education is a theory of practice. Successful teachers of low achievers send positive invitations to themselves and their students. To send an invitation always involves a risk. The invitation may not be accepted. Often the low-achiever has been disinvited—ignored and/or rejected—in so many ways that it is difficult to accept invitations. Effective teachers are aware of this reality and do not give up on the student.

The inviting stance of the successful teacher may be described in this way:

HOLD YOUR POINT! Champion bird dogs are judged in part by how long they "hold the point" when they detect a covey of birds. Similarly, champion teachers are judged by the way they consistently and dependably send invitations to students. Creating a positive classroom environment is a marathon, not a sprint. (112)

Studies confirm that students who are having difficulties in school often have poor self-concepts (115, 110, 25). Teachers can use strategies designed to increase the self-esteem of the low achiever. Felker suggests five principles for teachers who would like to foster healthy self-concepts in students:

- Praise yourself to set a model for self-reinforcement for accomplishments.
- Help students to evaluate themselves realistically.
- Teach students to set reasonable goals.
- Teach students to praise themselves.
- Teach students to praise others. (46)

27

Thus teachers who are successful with low achievers send positive invitations to themselves and their students. They are warm, caring, and nurturing, and they create places where students will want to learn. The classroom environment is inviting. Teachers take the extra time to make their rooms attractive with colorful bulletin boards, plants, student collections, posters, projects, and work displayed. They convey an excitement for learning. High school students describe inviting teachers in this way:

> "Mrs. A. was the best teacher I ever had....When you had problems, you could always go to her. Other teachers just yell at you when you don't understand something; they tell you to bring a note home to your parents."

> "Mr. M. has the ability to create an atmosphere where you don't feel scared to ask a question. Even if you feel dumb, he doesn't make you look dumb by asking the question in class or by saying, 'I really don't understand'."

> "Mr. N. was a teacher you could really talk to. He listened to you, and he helped you to learn because he didn't shoot you down when you asked a question." (36)

Expanding on the earlier work of Carl Rogers, Aspy and Roebuck support the philosophy of invitational education in extensive studies. They conclude that the higher the levels of understanding, genuineness, and respect a teacher gives students, the greater the likelihood that students will learn (5). Thus, inviting practices by teachers lead to positive student outcomes. The time teachers spend building positive rapport with students, particularly those at risk, can be well justified. Inviting educators reap the reward of improved student performance because of their emphasis on the whole child.

Collegial Learning

> The nature of the relationships among the adults who inhabit a school has more to do with the school's quality and character and with the accomplishments of its pupils than any other factor. (10)

To meet the needs of low-achievers, teachers must collaborate. Many times a team approach is necessary to plan effective programs for these students who are at risk of failing and dropping out (150). High student achievement is more likely in schools with high faculty morale and a sense of shared responsibility (13, 34, 41, 47).

The premise that people working together toward a common goal can accomplish more than those working by themselves is an established principle of social psychology. An extensive review of the research encompassing 90 years and 450 studies is summarized by Johnson and Johnson. These researchers found that cooperation among adults promotes achievement, positive interpersonal relationships, social support, and positive self-esteem. They conclude that organizing teachers and administrators into collegial support groups should result in greater productivity and expertise, more positive interpersonal relationships and cohesion among the faculty, and enhanced self-esteem for the educators (76). To achieve these positive results, collegial groups should be structured following specific procedures.

Some schools are organized to isolate teachers. Lortie refers to the "cellular" nature of the school that prevents teachers from working together (92). Because of this, most teachers concentrate on the instructional skills they can employ alone rather than the skills that could be developed in close cooperation with others (57).

Teachers who have made commitments to improve the education of low achievers, however, create environments that allow them to work collegially. Sometimes this requires a great deal of innovation on the part of both teachers and administrators. In some schools principals form study groups and teachers plan curriculum improvements in areas of targeted interest. The principal hosts morning coffees, wine and cheese parties, or after-school teas to get the staff involved and working together. Professionals are allowed to leave school early on some days and make up the time on other days. This is a trade-off and a philosophy that respects the rights of teachers as professionals. It clearly communicates to teachers a valuing of their talent and the importance of sharing, caring, and flexibility.

Another added benefit of collegiality is that teachers find positive ways to handle stress. Research on stress management emphasizes the value of team development in dealing with the many demands of teaching. Some of the benefits of this technique include the following: sharing ideas for dealing with stress, developing team teaching to reduce the negative effects of stress, forming human support systems that enhance teacher self-concepts, and developing teacher centers where personal and professional sharing can take place on a continuous basis. Team approaches can be initiated through faculty planning groups; they can take many forms, including study groups, in-service education teams, and team planning groups (137).

Schools that have promoted ways for teachers to work together and provide time for collegial planning and problem solving have found a new vitality and excitement among the staff that energizes the learning climate of the school (140).

Positive Discipline

Both teachers and students need a safe and orderly learning environment. Students who are at risk tend to be discipline problems (96, 44, 26). Behavioral and academic success go together (143). Teachers who are most effective with low achievers have a classroom management plan that clearly delineates behavioral expectations. These teachers also clearly communicate classroom expectations to parents. Many potential problems can be prevented by close communication and understanding between teachers and parents.

Some teachers have found the model of assertive discipline developed by Lee Canter (26) particularly effective. The model consists of three parts, each of which is critical to the success of the management plan. First, classroom rules should be clearly stated. Sometimes low achievers are confused by mixed signals regarding what is considered appropriate behavior. The class rules should clearly and positively communicate to students the needs of the teacher without infringing in any way upon the dignity of the students. The second part of Canter's model outlines the consequences of a student's choosing to break a class rule. These should be realistic, comfortable for the teacher to enforce, and respectful of the rights of the student. With the rules and consequences clearly stated, the teacher employs the third part of the model, the positive reinforcement plan. This includes the many motivational strategies, both individual and classwide, the teacher will use in reinforcing appropriate behavior. The critical factor in determining whether assertive discipline works depends on this part of the plan. Assertive discipline is not a panacea and may not be appropriate for all classrooms. It has raised considerable controversy and has definite limitations. It is discussed here as only one possibility, not the only one.

Students who are at risk in school often have not learned to accept responsibility for their own behavior. To address this problem, some successful dropout prevention programs require a commitment from students to a set of rules, work expectations, and standards of behavior. Clear rules and consequences need to be spelled out in detail. Once students accept program requirements and goals, discipline problems can be expected to decline (150).

With students who often misbehave, the effective teacher searches for the underlying reason and seeks help to develop appropriate intervention strategies. Swick suggests these warning signals to teachers:

1. A drastic change in a student's behavior or routine may indicate a change in the life context of that student. A child who is normally outgoing and who suddenly becomes withdrawn is usually signaling for help.

2. A student who exhibits extreme behavior indices usually has some dysfunction in terms of human functioning. For example, an extremely aggressive child needs immediate attention and assistance in reorganizing her or his behavior. A child who is very listless may be telling the teacher that she or he is abused, malnourished, or not getting proper rest or attention at home. Do not allow these extremes to go unattended; they can develop into severe discipline problems.

3. A student who is always unprepared, constantly disorganized, and generally unable to handle basic classroom routines is indicating to the teacher that she or he is in need of "organizational help." Such a student, if allowed to continue in this manner, will eventually have a negative effect on other students and generate other problems for herself or himself and the teacher.

4. A student who is unable to accept even the most basic authority limits necessary for classroom management should receive immediate attention. The "I-don't-have-to-do-that" syndrome can create a climate of chaos in the classroom and will only have negative effects on everyone involved.

5. The student and the teacher who have role conflicts and/or personality clashes early in the school year are, if left unattended, headed for more severe problems later in the school year! The teacher, upon recognizing such a situation, needs to examine his or her part in the conflict as well as assessing the student's part. By resolving the problem early in the school year, everyone can have a more productive learning experience. (136)

To summarize, then, teachers who are effective classroom managers of low achievers—

- develop a positive discipline plan with rules, consequences, and reinforcement strategies.
- communicate closely with parents.
- strive to get a behavioral commitment from students.
- get help in planning intervention strategies for chronic behavioral problems.

Cooperative Learning

How can the teacher structure the learning environment so that the low achiever can succeed? An effective method is through a form of group learning referred to as cooperative or student-team learning. This is an instructional method in which students of all performance levels work together in small groups toward a common goal.

Cooperation is an important human activity. According to research findings, however, this is a skill in which many low-achieving students need help (56, 74, 128). So often teachers tell students to "get along" or "cooperate" but spend little time on skill practice and discussion of this basic human need. It is the teacher who determines the interaction patterns of students within the classroom. Cooperative learning provides the teacher with a model to improve academic performance and socialization skills, and to instill democratic values. A wealth of research supports the idea that the consistent use of this technique improves students' academic performance and helps them become more caring (39, 161, 128, 99, 127, 73, 125). Slavin summarizes the effectiveness of cooperative learning as follows:

> The research on cooperative learning methods supports the usefulness of these strategies for improving such diverse outcomes as student achievement at a variety of grade levels and in many subjects, intergroup relations, relationships between mainstreamed and normal-progress students, and student self-esteem. Their widespread and growing use demonstrates that in addition to their effectiveness, cooperative learning methods are practical and attractive to teachers. The history of the development, evaluation, and dissemination of cooperative learn-

ing is an outstanding example of educational research resulting in directly useful programs that have improved the educational experience of thousands of students and will continue to affect thousands more. (126)

Teachers who wish to succeed with all students should consider implementing cooperative learning. Two excellent models now available provide specific procedures: Student Team Learning Methods from The Johns Hopkins University developed by Robert E. Slavin (125, 122) and Cooperative Learning developed by David and Roger Johnson (73) at the University of Minnesota.

THE ROLE OF THE PARENTS

The Importance of the Parents

Parents can play a major role in helping the underachieving student. Research indicates that during the formative years—until the end of high school—parents nominally control 87 percent of a student's waking time (148). The attitude that parents convey to their children about the importance of learning is a major variable in student success. Students who believe in the value of hard work and responsibility and who attach importance to education are less likely to become school dropouts (51).

Because the curriculum of the home predicts learning twice as well as the socioeconomic status of families (148), the importance of parent education is paramount in succeeding with low-achieving students. Effective schools appreciate the absolute necessity of getting parents involved in the educational program. This is often not an easy task. In some cases, parents of low achievers distrust the school system, based on their individual anxieties caused by previous negative experiences. If fewer parents are intimidated or excluded from the work of the school, children at risk will have added resources and schools will have more allies (33).

Getting Parents Involved

Many times the first step in parent involvement can be taken by the classroom teacher through a home visit. Teachers who have been most effective in getting disinvited parents (those who have been ignored and/or rejected) involved in the educational program use this strategy. When visiting the home, teachers might consider the following suggestions:

- Communicate positively to parents about their child (in some cases parents have heard only negatives).
- Explain classroom expectations.
- Talk about the importance of the curriculum of the home in learning and what parents can do—for example, talking with their child about everyday events, encouraging and modeling reading, expressing affection and interest in their child's academic and personal growth, limiting television time.
- Delineate ways the parents can help their child, such as setting aside a definite time every day for homework, providing a quiet place to work, listening to their child read, signing class contracts and papers.
- Answer any questions the parents might have about the educational program.
- Invite parents to visit and/or help in the classroom, to attend parent training seminars, to come to an open house or parent teacher meeting.

As one teacher remarked, "The most valuable strategy I have learned in 25 years of teaching is the importance of making a home visit. It establishes a positive rapport we build on the entire school year" (85). Some school principals work with classroom teachers to arrange schedules and/or released time to facilitate home visits to talk with parents of low achievers.

A comprehensive study of 3,698 teachers reported that fewer than one quarter of those surveyed indicated that they had made any home visits during the school year, and only 2 percent said they had visited more than a handful of children's homes (11). Getting parents involved as partners in the educational process is a valuable technique but it is being used by very few educators.

What Can Happen

Programs that target parent/teacher cooperation and focus on specific goals show the greatest learning effects. In one inner-city school, staff members and parents formulated specific goals such as

"Increasing parents' awareness of the reading process," and designed ways to involve the community in achieving the goal. The success of the program shows that inner-city children can make middle-class progress in achievement if educators work cooperatively with parents in pursuit of joint goals (148).

A project called Home Start had obvious success in meeting the needs of economically deprived families. A major feature of this federally funded program was to send teachers to the home of parents to educate them on ways they could help their children develop physically, emotionally, socially, and intellectually (59).

The New Parents as Teachers Project in Missouri has been targeted as a national model for parental involvement in dropout prevention programs. Parent volunteers, numbering some 34,000 families in 1987, represent all income levels and family types. The program provides continuing service from the third trimester of pregnancy until the child reaches age three. Services include education in the home on child development, meetings with other parents, and a parent resource center with appropriate learning materials (144).

Clearly, the message is understood. Virtually every effective program for dropout prevention, low achievers, underachievers—all students at risk—contains innovative components of parent involvement. Parents must be equal partners in educational improvement.

Chapter 3

INVOLVING AT-RISK STUDENTS IN LEARNING

Tell me—I forget
Show me—I remember
Involve me—I understand
—Chinese Proverb

Research suggests two conditions under which teachers can increase the degree of student involvement in learning: instructional processes and motivational strategies.

INSTRUCTIONAL PROCESSES

Educational research now offers teachers a number of processes that will increase the probability of student learning. This chapter reviews the processes that have been found particularly effective for at-risk students. Effective implementation of the processes is of course essential to attain the maximum benefit for students.

Teachers of low achievers need to present information in a variety of ways and build into the curriculum methods that students can use to process the information. Classrooms that increase the likelihood of students' learning and retaining concepts are information processing as opposed to information receiving. That is, after teachers present the facts, students become involved in their learning with hands-on experiences. In a unit on aerodynamics, for example, students could construct and fly model airplanes as a culminating activity. The more actively involved low achievers become in their learning, the greater the likelihood that it will have meaning, retention, and transfer. The goal is to help students process information in meaningful ways in order to become independent learners. According to Goodlad (58):

> If students are to learn, they must become engaged with the subject matter, whether it is a mathematical problem, the characteristics of some other culture, the shaping of clay, or the structure of a poem. This engagement does not occur similarly for all kinds of learning; nor does it occur similarly for all individuals, whatever the subject matter. A concept needs to be read about, talked about, written about, perhaps danced or acted out, and eventually used in some meaningful context.

Research on low achievers suggests that instruction that is interactive and requires students to use several modalities increases achievement gains (132). Teachers must first get the learner started, keep the learner involved, and then determine the learner's success.

Getting the Learner Started

In general, research findings demonstrate that slow learners take much more time to get started on learning activities than do their faster-learning peers (88). Effective teachers of low achievers give students the appropriate tools they will need to complete the learning tasks. Very often this entails helping students learn how to learn. For example, many low achievers need direct teaching of study skills. They do not know how to outline, how to listen, or how to organize their materials. Effective teachers clearly state their expectations for students and then demonstrate (i.e., model) expected starting behaviors. Jones uses the term *mediator* to describe the teacher's role:

> As a mediator, the strategic teacher intercedes between the students and the learning environment to help students learn and grow, anticipates problems in learning and plans solutions to solve them, and guides and coaches students through the initial phase of learning to independent learning. (79)

Mediating teachers, then, make no assumptions about what skills the student brings to the learning; they consider all the variables and teach accordingly. The following pages describe several ways that teachers can help at-risk students develop the skills they need to become involved in their learning—teaching study skills, and using kindling, advance organizers, and mnemonics.

Study Skills

Research confirms that successful students know how to study. Many poor achievers fail in school, not because they lack intellectual ability, but because they do not know how to organize and assimilate information (91).

At-risk students are often assigned seatwork that they do not understand; therefore they devise inappropriate ways to complete the assignment. Anderson, who has done extensive research in this area, suggests that—

> Poor seatwork habits developed in the first grade may contribute to the subsequent development of a passive learning style. Low achievers, who often work on assignments they do not understand, may come to believe that schoolwork does not have to make sense, and that, consequently, they do not need to obtain additional information or assistance. (2)

Successful teachers use a variety of techniques to get low achievers off to a positive start. For example, they—

- teach the needed study skills.
- give students training in self-monitoring techniques.
- tape a card inside the student's desk with a checklist of assignments.
- assist the student in setting and completing realistic goals.
- utilize an attention getter when beginning a lesson.
- give clear directions, model expected behavior, and have selected students model the behavior.
- have students select a peer when they need help.
- ask low achievers in a nonjudgmental way to repeat the instructions.
- monitor seatwork carefully.
- have students use "help cards" at their desk to signal when they need assistance.
- specify the amount of work and delineate time limits for its completion.
- utilize pre-tests to know the appropriate place to begin instruction.

Kindling

A technique that increases the likelihood that low achievers will get involved in learning is the process of kindling. This five-step procedure is designed to help students consider and develop an idea before a class discussion (134). It builds in time for thinking and interacting with peers before students respond. The five steps of kindling are as follows:

- The teacher presents the question such as, "What are the attributes of a good thinker?"
- Students individually write a response to the question. Younger children can draw a picture.
- Each student shares the answer with a partner. The teacher encourages students to listen to their partner's answer and see if, working together, they want to expand their response.
- Students discuss the question in small groups. Each person shares ideas and the group expands the answer.
- The whole group is now ready for a discussion because the idea has been kindled.

This process will improve the quality of class discussions and in many cases get the low achiever involved. S/he might be secure enough to speak up in class because of writing an answer, sharing it with a partner, and discussing the question in a small group.

Advance Organizers

As defined by Ausubel, advance organizers characterize material to be learned at a higher level of abstraction, generality, and inclusiveness (6). Ausubel is not suggesting that advance organizers should be highly abstract or difficult to understand. On the contrary, to be useful, they should be stated in terms familiar to the learner (7). Ausubel points out that organizers are especially useful when the material to be learned is not well organized and the learners are of limited ability and thus likely not to have the skills to organize the materials themselves. Of the more than 200 studies conducted on the value of advance organizers, researchers have differed on their findings. During the last few years, however, this technique has advanced, and many current reviewers are positive. In fact, Rolheiser-Bennett's review of 18 research investigations on their use concludes that "the average student studying with the aid of organizers learns about as much as the 90th percentile student studying the same material without the assistance of the organizing ideas" (81).

The use of advance organizers aids many students in moving from concrete operations to more formal operations. Examples of advance organizers that teachers have used with low achievers follow. (See Figures 1, 2, and 3.)

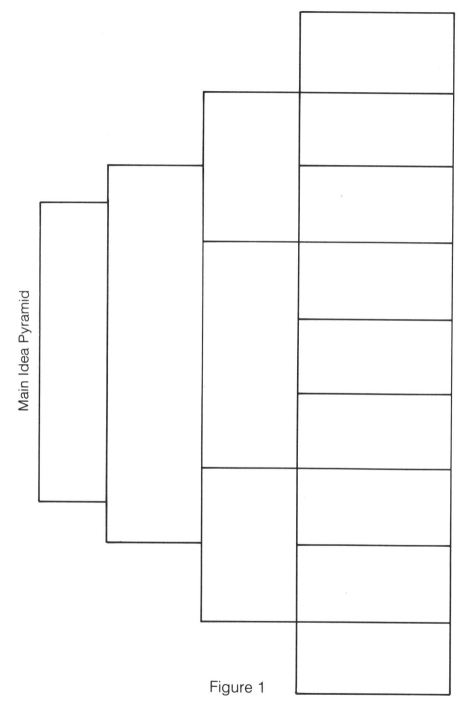

Main Idea Pyramid

Figure 1

Cause

Effect

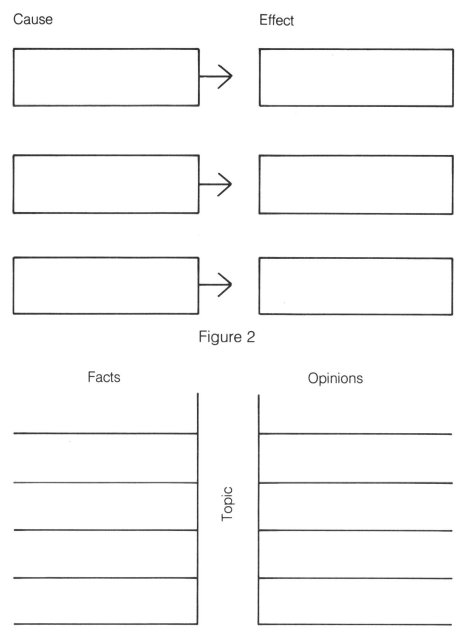

Figure 2

Facts

Opinions

Topic

Figure 3

Mnemonic Devices

Most people can commit to memory only small bits of information at a time. When students are given a series of items to remember, they tend to remember those at the beginning and the end. The mind seems to search for cues that will help it remember information (130). It remembers best with a mnemonic device, a memory trick that uses a repetitive pattern or association (89). For example, to help students learn to spell the word "geography," teachers have used this mnemonic: George Edison's oldest girl rode a pig home yesterday. (Also see the Appendix for an example of a mnemonic for metric conversion.)

Low achievers especially need extra tricks to help them remember. Songs, mottoes, and rhymes, for example, can be very helpful. When teaching numbers, the use of rhyming words can make them easy to learn—one/run, two/zoo, three/tree. Visualization techniques also can be helpful in assisting memory. Students might close their eyes and create a mental picture of the number one running. They might also write the number in the air as a kinesthetic/tactile hook.

Research confirms that at-risk students need clear structure and help to develop hooks on which they can hang new information (132). The use of advance organizers and mnemonics helps students remember this material. These techniques are also motivating to learners. Considering the variety of student learning styles in the classroom, it is important to teach to all modalities—auditory, visual, tactile/kinesthetic—in order to facilitate mastery.

Keeping the Learner Involved

Once teachers have gotten students started on learning activities, they need to ensure that they will remain involved. The strategies described in the following pages—using questions, technology, educational games and simulations, and the newspaper—can help to achieve this involvement.

Questioning

Stimulating, thought-provoking questions are the glue that holds the instructional program together. Research indicates a positive relationship between frequency of academic questions addressed to students and gain in student achievement (23). A review of the literature shows that the following suggestions for questioning techniques are well supported by many studies (56, 121, 138, 45, 113, 133).

- Structure questions so that students can succeed. (Achievement was maximized with low-socioeconomic-status children when they answered about 80 percent of questions correctly.)

- Encourage students to respond. (Most teachers answer two-thirds of their own questions.)

- Ask questions in all modes. (Most questions are asked at basic recall or recognition level. More complex questioning increases student achievement.)

- Pause—the number and quality of student answers increase when teachers provide "wait time" of three to five seconds after asking a question and before the student responds. Appropriate wait time is particularly important in teaching low achievers. Some higher-level questions might require fifteen to twenty seconds of wait time.

- Call on students randomly, but be sure not to forget the low achiever. Attention is better when teachers are unpredictable in their pattern of calling on students. In small groups with low-socioeconomic-status students, more structure is sometimes desirable, however, and teachers use a patterned method—going around the small circle—more effectively.

- When a student responds incorrectly, point out what is incorrect and rephrase the question to elicit an improved response.

- If a student's response is vague, call for clarification or elaboration—for example, "Tell me more." Probe students to higher levels of thinking.

- Respond to correct answers with positive body language (nod the head) or short affirmation statements.

- In general, praise is more successful in improving the achievement of students less accustomed to success and in need of encouragement.

- Encourage students to develop and ask their own questions. (This will increase their opportunities for thinking.)

- Utilize techniques that require students to use their own questions and to make discoveries on their own. For example, in a science lesson ask students to make predictions, based on their own experiences, prior to a demonstration or experiment. In a lesson of this type the processes of observing, comparing, and describing are as important as the product.

When improving their questioning strategies in the classroom, teachers might want to consider tape-recording the discussion. Listening to a tape and evaluating one's performance is an effective way to do this. Another method to improve this skill is to work with another teacher as peer tutors—coaching each other to use more effective questioning techniques.

Technology

Today's technology, especially the microcomputer, has the potential for improving both the delivery of instruction and the management of learning. At this point in the development of educational technology, the computer seems to have the capability of providing educational benefits for the hard-to-teach, low-achieving student. It is probably also safe to say, however, that technological innovations will continue to be used as tools to improve the effectiveness of teachers, not to replace them (29, 82). The microcomputer can motivate students and individualize instruction. It can provide immediate feedback to users, while remaining nonjudgmental. It can give the learner autonomy—a quality missing in the lives of many students, especially those at risk. It can provide simulations that are useful in mathematics, science, and social studies. It can also provide simulated experiences to supplement, and, in some cases, replace laboratory work. Through the computer, students can become active generators of knowledge rather than passive consumers of information (68).

More and more examples of success stories involve the use of computers with at-risk students. One such story comes from Pensacola, Florida. The Escambia County School District established a remedial reading program for disadvantaged high school students who were below grade level in reading and mathematics. Using Computer Curriculum Corporation System software, the program showed impressive results—one month's growth in reading or mathematics for every hour the student spent on the system (68).

Educational Games and Simulations

Educational games and simulations also offer interesting possibilities for teachers of at-risk students. They allow teachers to create a structured, student-centered learning environment that can contribute to both the affective and cognitive growth of students. Moreover, games serve as motivational devices for students who have long ago lost interest in more conventional approaches to learning.

Teachers frequently design their own simulation games to fit content and course objectives while meeting the needs of special groups of students. The following ten steps were suggested by a professional game designer for teachers and others when designing a game for classroom use:

1 Define overall *objectives* (teaching, analysis, design, tests, exploration, etc.).

2. Determine *scope* (duration, geographic area, issues).

3. Identify key *actors* (individual groups or organizations making the critical decisions).

4. Determine *actors' objectives* (power, wealth, influence, etc., in specific contexts.

5. Determine *actors' resources* (physical, social, economic, political, information).

6. Determine the *interaction sequence among the actors* (flow of resources and information to and from each actor).

7. Determine the *decisions rules* or criteria on the basis of which actors decide what resources and information to transmit or receive or what actions to take.

8. Identify *external constraints* on actions of the actors (such as no violence being permitted in a competition among Quakers).

9. Formulate *scoring rules* or *win criteria* on the basis of the degree to which actors or teams of actors receive their objectives with efficient utilization of resources.

10. Choose form of presentation and manipulation (board game, role play, paper/pencil exercise, computer simulation), and formulate *sequence of operations*. (64)

The Newspaper

The newspaper can be an effective tool for use with low achievers who often have little interest in learning from more traditional materials. It is used most frequently to develop basic skills and to promote learning in a variety of subject areas. The newspaper's greatest appeal for many teachers is its use to improve students' reading skills, while providing an obvious up-to-date text for the social studies classroom (65).

Students who need a hands-on approach—as do many at-risk students—can benefit from numerous strategies that use the newspaper. For example, they can cut and paste spelling words, find examples of prefixes and suffixes, circle the parts of speech, and cut out examples of propaganda techniques. Additional strategies for using the newspaper can be found in the Appendix.

Determining the Learner's Success

How well have students learned? How close have they come to meeting the course objectives? What progress has Chris, Will, or Alice made? Questions such as these are frequently asked by teachers of low-achieving students.

Evaluation is a technical aspect of instruction. It is the part of the teaching-learning process that provides continuous feedback to keep the system in adjustment and balance (9). Tests, observational reports, anecdotal records, sociograms, collections of students' work, class diaries, committee reports, logbooks, and teacher-made tests are all types of evidence upon which evaluation is based. In the final analysis, however, evaluation is a judgmental act. The teacher's task, then, is (1) to formulate goals that are clear and precise, (2) to set criteria that are appropriate and attainable, (3) to gather data about the instructional process that is as accurate and objective as possible, and finally (4) to report that information to students, parents, and administrators in ways that are clear and meaningful (9).

While formal measures, such as objective tests, attitude surveys, and standardized tests, are important means of gathering data about students, they should not preempt the less formal methods that are readily at hand—the anecdotal record and the checklist of individual progress, for example. These two tools are especially useful to the teacher of low achievers, since these students frequently have a history of failure on more formal evaluation instruments (9). Homework, too, can provide teachers with information about student progress.

Anecdotal Records

An anecdotal record is a continuous log or diary of a student's progress written in a free-flowing, narrative form. It allows the teacher to add considerable detail about a student, particularly of a diagnostic nature. One danger of anecdotal reporting is the tendency of teachers to become subjective by including personal feelings about student behavior. When carefuly prepared, however, the anecdotal record offers a good source of data about at-risk students (9).

Checklists

Another simple measure for gathering data on instruction is the checklist. In essence, this is an abbreviated form of the objectives developed for a given unit as the teacher makes plans for instruction. The checklist gives a good record of a student's performance on a variety of objectives at different levels, and it is helpful when assessing both student and class progress. It enables the teacher to see at a glance which parts of a unit of work have been mastered and which have not. A combined checklist for the entire class can form the basis for reteaching a lesson. A word of caution—when using checklists, teachers should be sure to interpret the progress of individuals in terms of objectives accomplished, not as ''high'' or ''low'' compared with the entire class (9).

Homework

One way to help the low achiever keep up with classroom expectations is by assigning homework. Extra studying helps students of all ability levels.

A review of empirical studies of homework shows that the assignment and grading of work done at home produces an effect on achievement that is three times as large as family socioeconomic status (as indexed by parental income, education, and occupation). The reviewer concludes that ''homework produces uniformly positive effects on the factual, conceptual, critical and attitudinal aspects of learning'' (148).

Despite the evidence supporting the benefit of homework, it is often not optimally used in many schools. According to data analysis from Coleman's study *High School and Beyond*, during the school year American high school students average four hours of homework and 30 hours of television per week (155). Because it is difficult for homework to compete with television, teachers should perhaps consider using television as part of a homework assignment. For example, in a social studies class studying fact and opinion, the teacher could assign groups of students to view the evening news, searching for concrete examples of fact and opinion.

Researchers have also found that students in the United States spend less time doing homework than students in any country in Western Europe; that the top 5 percent of U.S. students do less homework than the average Japanese student; and that 44 percent of 17-year-old students surveyed in the United States reported having no homework assigned—or not doing their assignment (66).

One study revealed that when low-ability students complete just one to three hours of homework a week, their grades are usually as high as those of average-ability students who do not do homework. Similarly, when average-ability students do three to five hours of homework a week, their grades usually equal those of high-ability students who do no homework (143).

Perhaps a clearer understanding of homework is needed. Possible objectives could include the following:

- Giving extra practice needed for skill mastery
- Providing activities not possible in the classroom
- Saving instructional time
- Extending classroom learning
- Developing habits for effective use of leisure time.

Educators suggest the following strategies to increase the effectiveness of homework (66):

- Be sure that students have prerequisite skills for homework.
- Give homework at which students can succeed.
- Give clear, concise directions.
- Discuss the purpose and evaluation of assignments.
- Establish a schoolwide homework policy including procedures for makeup and lateness and consequences of failure to complete.

- Communicate the homework policy to parents and students.
- Enforce the homework policy consistently.
- Be flexible.
- Show students examples of successful assignments.
- Let students help design homework.
- Give "kickoff" help when necessary.
- Correct and comment on all assignments or have peers assist in grading.
- Solicit student feedback.
- Go easy on drill-type homework.
- Vary long- and short-term assignments.
- Plan with other teachers to avoid unfair assignments.
- Be sure that homework assignments consider the level and pace at which individual students complete their work.
- Design a homework assignment notebook for each student. This especially will help the low achiever.

MOTIVATIONAL STRATEGIES

"What can I do? Johnny isn't motivated to learn. Susie just sits in the back of the room totally apathetic. No matter what I do, Sam won't complete his homework. Help!" Teachers almost universally are asking this question. The challenge of how to motivate students to learn is one faced by all educators, but especially by teachers of low achievers.

A review of the literature provides numerous definitions, theories, and models of motivation. Psychologists disagree on definitions of motivation or its importance in the learning process. From our practical experience, however, we believe that the ability to help students want to learn is the foundation for success with low achievers. Abilities and skills are useless without the desire to use them. As Frymier observes, "Motivation is the driving force which assumes that opportunity, ability, and skill will result in better performance and deeper understanding" (49). The last two sections describe the work of two researchers in this area.

Brophy's Research

In an extensive review of the literature on motivational theory and the nature of learning, Brophy identifies 33 principles for motivating students (see p. 51). Based on sound research, these principles are suitable for application by teachers in the classroom.

These principles can be used to teach at-risk students in the following ways:

1. Supportive environment
Effective schools research indicates that low-achieving students need a safe positive environment that only the teacher can create. Students need to feel comfortable to take a risk without fear of failing.

2. Appropriate level of challenge/difficulty
Low achievers are reinforced when they experience success on appropriately challenging material. The curriculum need not be watered down for these students.

3. Meaningful learning objectives
Material should be relevant to the world of the low achiever. Students are more likely to achieve the learning objectives if they can see the meaning and reason for mastery.

4. Moderation/optimal use
Any motivational strategy can lose its effectiveness if used routinely. Changes in structure and pattern help keep the low achiever stimulated.

5. Program for success
Build success into the instructional program. Start where the student is and move at an appropriate pace, preparing the low achiever for increasing levels of difficulty.

6. Teach goal-setting, performance appraisal, and self-reinforcement skills.
Help students set realistic goals that are specific and challenging. Detailed feedback from the teacher helps low achievers to evaluate their progress.

7. Help students to recognize linkage between effort and outcome.
Low achievers often have difficulty understanding that what they get out of a learning activity is equal to the effort they are willing

50

Highlights of Research on Strategies for Motivating Students to Learn*

Research on student motivation to learn indicates promising principles suitable for application in classrooms, summarized here for quick reference.

Essential Preconditions
1. Supportive environment
2. Appropriate level of challenge/difficulty
3. Meaningful learning objectives
4. Moderation/optimal use

Motivating by Maintaining Success Expectations
5. Program for success
6. Teach goal setting, performance appraisal, and self-reinforcement
7. Help students to recognize linkages between effort and outcome
8. Provide remedial socialization

Motivating by Supplying Extrinsic Incentives
9. Offer rewards for good (or improved) performance
10. Structure appropriate competition
11. Call attention to the instrumental value of academic activities

Motivating by Capitalizing on Students' Intrinsic Motivation
12. Adapt tasks to students' interests
13. Include novelty/variety elements
14. Allow opportunities to make choices or autonomous decisions
15. Provide opportunities for students to respond actively

16. Provide immediate feedback to student responses
17. Allow students to create finished products
18. Include fantasy or simulation elements
19. Incorporate game-like features
20. Include higher-level objectives and divergent questions
21. Provide opportunities to interact with peers

Stimulating Student Motivation to Learn
22. Model interest in learning and motivation to learn
23. Communicate desirable expectations and attributions about students' motivation to learn
24. Minimize students' performance anxiety during learning activities
25. Project intensity
26. Project enthusiasm
27. Induce task interest or appreciation
28. Induce curiosity or suspense
29. Induce dissonance or cognitive conflict
30. Make abstract content more personal, concrete, or familiar
31. Induce students to generate their own motivation to learn
32. State learning objectives and provide advance organizers
33. Model task-related thinking and problem solving.

51

* Jere E. Brophy, "Synthesis of Research on Strategies for Motivating Students to Learn," *Educational Leadership* 45, no. 2 (October 1987). Reprinted with permission of the Association for Supervision and Curriculum Development and Jere E. Brophy. Copyright © 1987 by the Association for Supervision and Curriculum Development. All rights reserved.

to put into the task. Encourage them to accept responsibility for their own learning.

8. Provide remedial socialization.
Sometimes low achievers are their own worst critics. They are frustrated easily and want to quit. By helping them attribute failure to the lack of effort or an inappropriate strategy rather than to lack of ability, teachers can help them become more responsible learners.

9. Offer rewards for good (or improved) performance.
Low-achieving students respond to rewards for successful performance and good behavior. The most successful reward system—long-term—focuses on student improvement rather than the reward itself.

10. Structure appropriate competition.
Many low achievers are frightened by competition. However, healthy competition focusing on improved performance gives the student an equal chance for success.

11. Call attention to the instructional value of academic activities.
Help students realize the purpose of learning—to prepare them for a productive life. Low achievers often see academic activities as imposed demands rather than opportunities.

12. Adapt tasks to students' interest.
Low achievers learn best when teaching procedures take advantage of what they care about and/or experience outside the classroom.

13. Include novelty/variety elements.
Use a variety of activities to appeal to low achievers, such as allowing them to select topics, projects, and assignments that appeal to their curiosity.

14. Allow choices or autonomous decisions.
Encourage students to choose from among alternatives. Low achievers' motivation increases when they can cooperate and actively participate in learning and in decisions about their learning.

15. Provide opportunities for students to respond actively.
At-risk students often are multisensory learners and need to be actively involved. Games, role playing, and simulations make student reaction and involvement an integral part of the learning process.

16. Provide immediate feedback to student responses.
Feedback is one of the primary means by which students realize their competence. The more immediate the feedback, the more likely the low achiever will be motivated to continue the task.

17. Allow students to create finished products.
Students respond positively to tasks that yield a finished product that they can model or display.

18. Include fantasy or simulation.
Motivation increases as students become more emotionally involved in the learning.

19. Incorporate game-like features.
At-risk students are motivated by learning assignments that are unique. Create game-like puzzles, test-yourself activities, or brain teasers.

20. Include higher-level objectives and divergent questions.
Students achieve more when teachers ask thought-provoking questions and insist on thoughtful answers.

21. Provide opportunities to interact with peers.
Teachers who structure peer learning encourage both intellectual and social growth for students.

22. Model interest in learning and motivation to learn.
Through their presence and behavior teachers are powerful role models. Much of what is known about coping with everyday situations is learned through modeling.

23. Communicate desirable expectations and attributions about students' motivation to learn.
Teachers need to communicate high expectations to all students.

24. Minimize students' performance anxiety during learning activities.
Because evaluation techniques represent failure, their use creates anxieties for low achievers. Teachers need to foster a supportive, nonthreatening environment.

25. Project intensity.
Teachers communicate the importance of the learning task both verbally and nonverbally. At-risk students are particularly aware of the teacher's attitude toward what is being taught.

26. Project enthusiasm.
Show interest in the learning by presenting projects and assignments with enthusiasm.

27. Induce task interest or appreciation.
Appeal to the interest of the low achiever by relating the present learning to previous learnings that have importance to the student.

28. Induce curiosity or suspense.
To increase the likelihood of student learning, present information in an interesting and dramatic way.

29. Induce dissonance or cognitive conflict.
When the topic is familiar, some students think they may know everything. Introduce contrasting or disturbing data and information to increase motivation for the task.

30. Make abstract content more personal, concrete, or familiar.
It is especially important when teaching low achievers to create hands-on, concrete experiences.

31. Induce students to generate their own motivation to learn.
Interest and involvement depend on the part the student plays in the learning activity.

32. State learning objectives and provide advance organizers.
Prepare students for the new learning by stating the objectives with clarity and providing a framework for organizing the material.

33. Model task-related thinking and problem solving.
When using cognitive modeling, teachers make the invisible learning visible by thinking out loud as they solve the problem.

Wlodkowski's Model (M.O.S.T.)

Another model program to explore when developing a motivational plan is the Motivational Opportunities for Successful Teaching (M.O.S.T.) program (160). This program identifies three critical periods in any learning event during which particular motivational strategies will have maximum impact on the learner:

Beginning—when the student enters and starts the learning process.

During—when the student is involved in the body or main content of the learning process.

Ending—when the student is finishing or completing the learning. (160)

Wlodkowski suggests that teachers consider six basic questions when planning for the motivation needs of their students:

1. What can I do to guarantee a positive student attitude for this activity?

2. How do I best meet the needs of my students through this activity?

3. What about this activity will continuously stimulate my students?

4. How is the affective or emotional climate for this activity a positive one for students?

5. How does this activity increase or affirm students' feelings of competence?

6. What is the reinforcement that this activity provides for my students?*

*From *The M.O.S.T. Program: Motivational Opportunities for Successful Teaching,* by Raymond J. Wlodkowski (Phoenix, Ariz.: Universal Dimensions, 1983). Reprinted with permission.

Chapter 4

TEACHING AT-RISK, LOW-ACHIEVING STUDENTS

A REPORT FROM ONE SUCCESSFUL PROJECT

The Furman University Center of Excellence addresses the need for improved preparation of teachers to teach low achievers in regular classroom settings (85). A major goal has been the identification of the necessary skills/competencies to teach at-risk students. A core of 220 outstanding classroom teachers (K-12) in the Greenville County School District (South Carolina) were identified by their school principals, area curriculum coordinators, and consultants as successful teachers of low achievers. A total of 156 of these teachers completed an open-ended survey identifying up to fifteen skills/competencies needed by teachers of low-achieving students. The skills/competencies subsequently were categorized into five major areas: Personal Skills/Competencies, Professional Skills/Competencies, Materials, Methods, and Learning Environment. The comments that follow are a sampling of the unedited responses of the participating teachers, arranged by category. The figure that follows each subcategory indicates that 10 percent or more of the teachers identified the particular characteristic.

Personal Skills/Competencies

Teachers of low-achieving students need to be—

1. Accepting (14%)
   "Accept each child as a person of worth, no matter what his level."

2. Caring, concerned, empathetic, loving, respecting, humanistic (68%)
   "I feel the greatest need for a teacher of low-achieving students is to care for her students as individuals."
   "I also let my students know that I am human and that I too make mistakes. I don't know it all. I'll try to find the answer if I don't know."

3. Enthusiastic and energetic (17%)

"ENERGY ... most of the children require constant motivation, stimulation ... each new class needs a 'fresh and peppy teacher'!"

"Spontaneity—show excitement and joy; it's highly contagious."

4. Humorous (18%)

"Humor—where would I be without it!"

"Have a sense of humor—sometimes it's the only thing that saves the day!"

5. Patient (75%)

"Patience—Patience—Patience!"

"Ability to practice unending patience."

6. An effective communicator with students and PARENTS (65%)

"The willingness to listen to children and the perception to hear what they are really saying."

"Work cooperatively with the parents of the low achiever explaining what is expected of them."

7. Creative (18%)

"Creative, new ways to do the same old thing."

"Creative and innovative approach to teaching."

8. Flexible (30%)

"Flexible—be ready (!) with two or three other ways to teach a concept ... not always easy, but ..."

"Flexibility—to be able to take a prepared lesson for the day and scrap it at a moment's notice to adapt to the needs of the students at that time."

Professional Skills/Competencies

Teachers of low-achieving students need to—

1. Be professional (reliable, punctual, dedicated) (14%)

"I model high learning expectations by starting the day on time and continuing with planned activities until the end of the school day."

"The teacher should hold him/herself personally responsible for overall achievement of the students."

2. Utilize resources from other teachers and community (11%)

"Often young teachers are afraid to admit to other teachers that they don't know what a particular child's problem is and how to reach him. They need a willingness to say, 'I don't know,' and ask for advice. After the problem has been pinpointed, they need the ability to share the load with coworkers. I'm best at teaching low achievers in the language arts. A coworker is best with math low achievers. We often switch off students. Be self-confident enough to ask for help.''

Materials

Teachers of low-achieving students need to—

1. Adapt materials to appropriate levels (14%)

   "Skills in preparing teacher-made materials to fit special skill needs.''

   "Ability to adapt 'average' materials and supplies to meet the needs of low achievers.''

2. Develop and utilize manipulatives (24%)

   "Ability to create and use concrete manipulatives.''

   "Low achievers often work better with manipulative experiences. Teachers should have knowledge in this area.''

3. Utilize a wide range and VARIETY of materials (50%)

   "A willingness to try new ideas and to search for new ideas to re-peat skills in a challenging way. Low achievers often get bored easily. Computers they love!''

Methods

Teachers of low-achieving students need to—

1. Possess organizational skills (47%)
   * Planning
   * Time Management
   * Record Keeping

   "Organized! Be able to overplan and plan well. Planning is the key to teaching low-achieving children. They must know at all times what to do. You must plan so that students do not need to say, 'What next?' but simply look on a contract, chart, or board to find out their next job.''

   "Organization as a person—in order that you can [have] five or six different things going on in the room at the same time and not let it bother you.''

2. Set realistic goals and objectives for students (high expectations) (66%)

   "Set goals for them that make them feel as 'smart' as the other groups."

   "Feel that they are capable of learning and push them to learn. Don't sell them short and don't allow them to feel this way."

3. Diagnose, prescribe, and evaluate students (formally and informally) (47%)

   "Ability to assess student needs in specific skill areas through formal, informal, and impromptu means."

   "The ability to find the starting point for a student at which he can be successful."

4. Make learning relevant (24%)

   "Involve students by relating learning to something familiar to them within their environment."

   "Explain, if possible, why they need to learn certain things. Help them to see the value of education."

5. Individualize instruction (31%)

   "Individuality—accept each child as he is and teach him at his own level, using his background, experiences, or capabilities as a basis for instruction."

   "Individualize program as much as possible."

6. Utilize small group instruction (16%)

   "Know how to group for instruction and be realistic as far as lesson preparations on the teacher's part. I've had four spelling groups in a class of 18 before!"

   "Knowledge of grouping methods and how to best utilize them."

7. Utilize a VARIETY of techniques and methods (87%)

   "Vary your methods—use worksheets, textbook, supplementary books, boardwork, etc."

   "A gigantic bag of tricks to teach the same skill in numerous ways."

   "Offer practice in weak modes or areas, while teaching or instructing in mode where child has strength."

   "The ability to sequence directions and materials into definite logical steps."

8. Reteach and give students time to practice the skill or concept. Meaningful repetition is essential (78%)

   "Ability to teach the same skill repeatedly without losing the student's attention."

"Present concepts in very small bits of information with excess reinforcement, practice, reteaching, and repetition."

"Repetition of skills—have them tell you what they are to do—many times they don't understand after lesson."

9. Know how to teach reading and language arts skills (28%)

"Ability to teach reading definition of words, definitions in context, details, fact/opinion, drawing conclusions, character analysis, affixes."

"Ability to develop and use appropriate language activities. Low achievers are often deficient in language."

10. Have a thorough knowledge of all content areas (25%)

"Content knowledge—at this level (6–8) I find my experience as a K–3 teacher in true fundamentals is very helpful."

"Knowledgeable background of all subject areas."

11. Have training in special education (17%)

"Knowledge of different handicaps and some idea of characteristics and screening techniques."

Learning Environment

Teachers of low-achieving students need to—

1. Be a "Cheerleader":
   - Be Positive (75%)
   - Use Motivational Strategies (23%)
   - Reward (23%)
   - Enhance self-concepts (45%)
   - Ensure successful experiences (30%)

   "Have a 'sack full' of good things to say—even if it has to be about the color of the student's shirt! They need praise, smiles, pats on the back (rewards, special days, games, stickers, etc.)."

   "Knowledge of varied motivational techniques."

   "Praise, praise, and more praise!"

   "Plan for success—i.e., structure tasks to make success likely."

2. Create a warm, inviting learning environment (15%)

   "Warm, inviting learning climate—a clean, orderly, attractive room communicates that the teacher is on top of things and cares about the learning in the room. A bulletin board does not take the place of relevant teaching but it and similar touches promote a positive image to the students."

3. Be firm, consistent, and fair in classroom management (64%)

"Make expectations and rules well defined, with consequences to children. Be consistent!"

"These children often have behavior problems:
1. Establish rules and penalties.
2. Make them clear to all students.
3. Enforce them with consistency.
4. Do not make idle and frequent threats.
5. Listen to both sides of a disagreement.
6. Make decisions fairly.

"Preface every confrontation with a positive remark about the student."

4. Consider the TOTAL CHILD (mental, physical and emotional) (30%)

"A concern for the total student—not just his English work, for example. It takes time, but if a teacher is truly concerned that the student's dog died or his tooth aches, he'll be more likely to work 'for the teacher' even if he isn't willing to work 'for himself'."

"Knowledge of subject—not just the basics; but the developmental process of how, not just what, the child learns."

"Knowledge of child development—the effects of poor prenatal care, poor nutrition, lack of 'quality time'—all are factors in the total picture of teaching a student who has little interest in education and who comes from a family that has little or less interest in education."

"Knowledge of different lifestyles—most teachers do not live on welfare or food stamps; yet many of my students do. I learned more from seeing where my students live than from any other experience. I appreciate the fact that learning about Julius Caesar is of little importance when there wasn't any hot water for the student to bathe with. Appealing to their dreams to escape poverty with a job—and the needed skills—is vital if I want to motivate them to succeed."

SUMMARY

Fifty percent or more of the 156 teachers who responded indicated that the following skills/competencies are needed to teach low-achieving students:

- Utilizing a variety of techniques and methods   87%

- Reteaching and giving students time to practice
  the skill   78%
- Being positive   75%
- Being patient   75%
- Being caring, concerned, empathetic, loving,
  respecting humanistic   68%
- Setting realistic goals and objectives
  (high expectations)   66%
- Being a firm, consistent, and fair classroom manager   64%
- Utilizing a wide range and variety of materials   50%

AFTERWORD

No learning environment or teaching strategy will work for all students, but research indicates that some have a higher probability of bringing about success with at-risk students than others. We suggest that these students be identified early during the formative years and that social and academic enrichment programs be implemented.

School-based models can make an important difference with low achievers. The principal must provide the leadership to create an inviting, supportive learning environment for staff and students. The key ingredient in successful programs for at-risk students, however, is the attitude of the classroom teacher. By communicating high expectations, utilizing a variety of effective teaching strategies, and emphasizing the development of the total child, the teacher can be successful with these students.

Despite the rather bleak picture that becomes evident when one examines the realities of school for many low achievers, the future is promising. Citizens across the country realize that the American way of life rests upon the foundation of equality for all. Public schools have played the role of society's great equalizer in the past, and educators and educational organizations are rising again to the challenge. For example, the National Education Association has established a dropout prevention program, "Operation Rescue" (101, 102). The Urban Superintendents' Network (142) has listed the dropout problem as a major concern. The U.S. Department of Education has target programs for at-risk students as a top priority (144). The Association for Supervision and Curriculum Development and the elementary and secondary principals' associations have passed resolutions supporting programs for students at risk. In addition, parents, concerned citizens, the corporate sector, and policymakers are joining educators in the fight to save the country's greatest natural resource—its children!

It is exciting to think that the day is coming when all children—whether from affluent suburb, urban ghetto, or rural school—will have an equal educational opportunity. This is not an impossible dream. Together, concerned citizens can make it happen.

APPENDIX

PRACTICAL STRATEGIES FOR AT-RISK, LOW-ACHIEVING STUDENTS

The strategies that follow can help teachers in their work with at-risk students. These strategies are grouped into six categories: Reading/Writing/Spelling, Social Studies, Science, Mathematics, Adaptable to All Subjects, and Motivation/Self-Concept.

READING/WRITING/SPELLING

Book-Sharing Questions

In addition to the who, what, where, when, and why questions that could be asked about a story, select several of the following questions to ask students:

1. If you were in the story, how would you feel?
2. If you were the author, how would you change the story?
3. If you were the main character, what would you do at the end of the story?
4. How would the story change if it took place where we live?
5. What other events could happen with the same character?
6. How would the story be different if the main character was someone else?

Bus Duty Reading

Let a child volunteer to read a favorite story to a group of bus students who arrive at school about the same time each morning. If the child brings a book, allow several days, if necessary, and share the reading responsibility with other students, duty teachers, and administrators. This strategy gives participating students a chance to read orally to their peers and lets children hear other teachers, students, and administrators read. Books and stories on tape may also be used. Children can gather in small groups around a tape player to listen to these stories.

Change the Meaning

After a lesson on antonyms, ask students to rewrite a sports story using antonyms so that the story turns out exactly opposite. Teachers will be pleased with the way this activity can increase interest in the lesson.

Creative Writing

As a class, have students write an open-ended story. At the writing center, ask individual students to copy the story and write their own ending, using word books if needed.

Handwriting

This activity provides a degree of independence for students with fine motor problems in handwriting. Have students copy the handwriting assignment from an overhead transparency projected on the screen. Children place the tranparency over their own work to check the correct use of lines, the alignment of letters, and spacing.

Homework That Works

At the beginning of the year explain to parents that the purpose of reading homework is to enable students to read fluently and with expression just as they talk in general conversation. Therefore, reading homework will consist of sentences and short stories that students have read in class. These sentences and/or stories will contain the vocabulary words they need to recognize instantly without any sounding out.

Ask parents to read the sentences to students and then have the students read the same sentences, trying to match the fluency and expression they have just heard. Also ask parents to positively reinforce students with verbal praise. As students become more confident, they will be able to read the sentences independently.

The same method can be used for a short story. The new vocabulary words may be underlined in each sentence. After students are proficient in reading the sentences, they can be asked to instantly identify the underlined words. A further drill is to write the new word on a card or a small piece of paper. On the reverse side of the card, students should write two or three sentences using the new word. If they hesitate to instantly identify the new word in isolation, they can turn the card over and read the word in context. These additional sentences also provide practice in fluent reading of new words in context.

Name That Noun

Number a series of pictures and hand out a different picture to several small groups of students. Ask each group to list all the nouns in the picture. Rotate the pictures. After all pictures have been circulated, compare the lists of nouns for each picture.

A Nickel for Mastery

Give each child an appropriate vocabulary list on Friday. By the following Friday, each child must recognize the words and make a sentence for each word, using the word correctly and showing its meaning. For students who master the list, place a nickel in individual baby food jars bearing their names. Students who do not master the list try again the following week. (Have parent volunteers check each student individually.) At the end of the year, students can spend the nickels they have earned on books at the school book fair.

Poetry Buffs

Each Monday introduce a poem for the week. Ask students to listen to and then read the poem together. Stress the rhyme and rhythm of the poem; discuss its author and relate it to other poems students know. If the poem is suitable, use it as a choral reading. Write the poem on a chart at the front of the room. Have the class read the poem together each day. By Friday many students will have it memorized. Have students copy the poem, illustrate it, and place it in their own poetry book. On special occasions, have the class perform for a nearby class or even the PTO by reciting some of their poetry.

Question of the Day

To help reluctant readers become more interested in reading, provide a new question for them to research every day or two. As students collect information to answer the day's question, they can share their information and their success with the class. Low achievers especially enjoy the success they feel as they find information. In the process, they also develop new library skills.

Rainbow Paragraphs

This is a very structured way to teach children to write a paragraph. Use the following key:

Green—Good start (opening sentence with three ideas)
Blue—Complete thought about first idea
Orange—Complete thought about second idea
Purple—Complete thought about third idea
Red—Good stopping sentence

Make a large poster as an example of a Rainbow Paragraph. Have students write first in pencil and then trace their writing with a magic marker. Or have students write their sentences and color the line below each sentence. The first time students write a rainbow paragraph, have them show their first sentence to you before you give them a green marker. Make sure they have named the three ideas—for example, instead of

I have three favorite TV shows.

the sentence should read:

My favorite TV shows are *The Cosby Show*, *Cheers*, and *Hill Street Blues*.

This is the hardest thing to get across with low achievers. Once they understand the idea, the rest is easy.

This technique helps students organize their thoughts. It is appropriate for science, social studies, reading, and language arts .

Read In

To promote the practice of positive leisure-time reading, set aside a specific time each day or week when everyone—principal, teachers, students, school employees—is enjoying reading.

Reluctant Readers—Sports Books

Coach Sandy Patlak has found that the interest of low achievers can be sparked by the right book. While troubled readers often shy away from reading subject matter, their attitude about sports is often enthusiastic. Patlak has developed a reading list entitled *Sandy's 99 Sports Books for Reluctant Readers*. It deals with books of upper-grade or junior high reading level on such topics as auto racing, baseball, basketball, boating, bowling, boxing, diving, football, tennis, and swimming. Many of the books are published by Scholastic.

Reluctant Readers—Use Radio Scripts

Students who have been turned off to reading can really get turned on by reading scripts of radio programs such as ''The Lone Ranger,'' ''Who's on First?''

Secret Observer

Place the name of each student in a jar. Ask each child to choose one name from the jar, keeping it a secret. All students observe the person whose name they have drawn for a week and keep a journal of the positive things that student has done. At the end of the week, students give their journal to that friend. (This activity requires discussion before and after it is completed.)

Sound Patterns

Choose a word containing a sound pattern that can be illustrated—for example, pig for /ig/, hat for /at/, cake for /ake/. Draw the pig, hat, or cake on poster board. Write the sound pattern below the picture. Staple several small strips of paper at the beginning of the sound pattern. Write a consonant on each strip to make a word. Rather than sound and blend several different sounds, the child can now blend only two sound units—the initial consonant and the pattern. The illustrated background gives a boost to get started on the first word.

Spelling—Alphabetizing

Cut off the front and back of a plastic notebook to use as a board. (Many companies discard old catalogs that can be used for this purpose.) Cut plastic dividers into rectangles to use as word cards. Glue velcro on the back of the rectangles and on the front of the board, so that the rectangles will adhere to the board. Using a washable felt marker or a grease pen, write a word on each rectangle and let the children arrange the words in alphabetical order before writing them. Use a damp rag to wipe off the words so that the cards can be used again.

Evaluation: This is a very effective way to reduce the frustration of writing, erasing, and rewriting. Children enjoy playing with the words and can write them once they have arranged them alphabetically.

Spelling Beans

Try playing spelling *beans* with dried lima beans. Write spelling words on the beans—one letter on each bean. When the ink dries, use clear nail polish to seal the letters. Place the beans for each word in separate baby food jars. Students go to the spelling center and select the jars containing the words they need to practice.

Spin-a-Yarn

Decorate a coffee can. Punch a hole in the center of the lid. Take a ball of yarn and tie knots in the yarn every three or four feet. Put the ball in the can with the end projecting from the hole in the lid. One person takes the end and starts a story while winding the yarn until a knot appears, then passes it to the next person who continues the story. Start with a *Main Idea* sentence. This activity helps children stick to the main idea as they provide supporting details.

$10 Sentence Time

Talk to students about the importance of writing in clear, interesting sentences (not "baby" sentences). Share many examples of good writing. Ask students to write their own sentences and share them orally. From time to time, ask students to mark their $10 sentence (the best sentence on their paper) with a star and share it with the class or with a neighbor. Ten-dollar sentence time will become an important time in the classroom. Students enjoy sharing their work!

69

Using the Newspaper

Ask students to use the newspaper for the following activities:

- Find as many compound words as you can from a page of the newspaper. Write them in your notebook and be ready to explain each word's contribution to the meaning of the new compound word.

- Write a want ad for something you would like to buy. Be concise and clear. Let a neighbor tell you whether he/she can correctly "picture" the object you are describing.

- Cut words from newspaper headlines and ads; mark the syllables.

- Find ten proper names in the newspaper. Put them in alphabetical order.

- Select three or four pictures from the newspaper. Write as many descriptive words as you can for each picture.

- Find as many words as you can from the newspaper that illustrate concepts of quality (for example, all silk, heavy duty).

Word Bank

Use any kind of container with a lid to serve as a Word Bank for each student to use at home. Paint each child's name (for example, John's Word Bank) on the container. As new vocabulary is introduced, print the words on a handout for students to take home, cut the strips apart, and add the words to their Word Bank for continuous review with Mom and Dad.

Write a Letter

Students go to a letter-writing center weekly and write a letter to a classmate. For evaluation, students check with the teacher before putting the letter in an envelope. By glancing quickly at the letter, the teacher can see if the student is using correct letter form. On Friday, the letters are delivered, and students may share them if they wish.

Write On

Set a definite time each week for schoolwide writing time. Select a student from each class as the weekly winner to receive a special certificate from the principal. From the winners that each teacher selects, the principal chooses two schoolwide winners—one for most creative and the other for most improved. Display all winning papers. Have students' pictures taken for the newspaper, and even encourage students to read their winning papers on the intercom or school news program.

SOCIAL STUDIES

Around the World in Ten Jumps

Divide the class into two teams. After the class has read the day's issue of the newspaper, a student from the first team names and locates a place on the map that was in the news. The second team then has one chance to guess why it was in the news. Continue in ten jumps around the globe until the teams return to the starting point. When a team makes a mistake or has had ten jumps, the other team has its turn.

Be a Newspaper Detective

Have students find items in the newspaper that represent fact, rumor, opinion, and propaganda. Ask them to find partners and share their findings.

Beat the Clock

Divide students into two groups and ask one person from each team to go to the chalkboard and write in one minute as many ideas (people, places, events) as possible from the assignment.

Community Crossword

1. Have students develop a crossword puzzle of community names, places, and events that have recently appeared in the newspaper. They should try to use at least 20 words. If they have problems in developing the puzzle, they can use words that are associated with their community but have not appeared in the newspaper recently.
2. Have students exchange puzzles with their classmates and solve them.

Community Obituary

Ask students to assume that their community is no longer in existence. As ridiculous as it may seem, the decision has been made to eliminate the community. Ask students to write an obituary for the community. Limit them to no more than 100 words.

Draw a Picture

Ask students to draw a picture or a diagram representing the main ideas they have read about in social studies or science. Give students opportunities to retell their ideas by using their picture or diagram.

Government Censorship

Have students examine the front page of a current newspaper. Ask them to cross out articles they think would not be allowed in the paper if government censorship existed. Have them share their finding with the class and explain why they selected their articles.

Headlines I'd Like to See

1. Ask students to examine the headlines in the daily newspaper and acquaint themselves with the way they are written.
2. Then have students think of some good news related to their community that they would like to see happen.
3. Ask students to write at least five headlines for their "good news" stories. They can clip words from regular newspaper headlines and paste them on a sheet of paper. Have students arrange the headlines in order of importance to them.

In a Nutshell

Appoint a daily news commentator who is responsible for a three-minute coverage of the day's news. Change reporters frequently and always make the assignment ahead of time so that the student can plan for success.

Inside the Brain

Cut out several headlines from the issue of the newspaper that has been delivered to the class for all students to read and place them in a paper bag. After quiet reading time, divide the class into teams. One team member pulls a headline from the bag and gives enough information to show that she/he has read the news story. A point for the team is scored if the class is satisfied that the student did read the story. Continue through the teams until all headlines have been used and each team has had an equal number of turns.

Interpreting Cartoons

Have the class interpret an editorial cartoon from the newspaper. Ask students to explain the purpose of an editorial cartoon. Then have them select an issue of relevance to them and draw their own editorial cartoons. Have students exchange and interpret each other's work.

Know and Don't Know

Introduce a new topic by asking students to make a list on newsprint of what ''they know'' and ''don't know'' about it. Keep the list and see if students know the answers at the end of their study. This exercise lets students know that it is perfectly all right not to have all the information about any topic.

Mock Interview

Ask students to select a personality in the news. Have them write a series of questions that they would like to ask the person if they met him/her. With the help of a friend, ask students to hold a mock interview with this person and answer the questions as they think the news personality would answer them.

Newspaper Advertising

Guide students in studying newspaper advertising. Using examples from the local newspaper, show the class a variety of techniques used in advertising. Note the words in the advertisements that influence the reader. Point out the action verbs, colorful adjectives, and types of figurative language found in a group of advertisements. Then have students create and design an original product. Ask them to give their product a name and design a newspaper ad to sell it. Low-achieving students respond to the freedom this activity gives them. Teachers find that these students can be very creative when given an opportunity.

Parade of Culture

As students study different countries, have them decorate shoe boxes as floats to show important aspects of the culture of each country.

Party Time

Plan, prepare for, and carry out a formal party or festival in the style of the country being studied. Use costumes, decorations, foods, and dances representative of the country.

Pick Out the New Words

As students read new material in social studies or science, ask them to write down all the new words they find. Have them write the meaning of the word that is implied through the context clues given in their reading. Follow with a brief class discussion to compare definitions before students look for a formal definition from the glossary of the textbook or a dictionary.

Pictorial Maps

After studying a unit in the social studies text, have students design a pictorial map of events to illustrate important ideas.

Role Play

Have students dramatize something important from a newspaper interview. The class must identify the person(s) and issue(s) involved. A discussion of the particular issue could follow. This kind of activity helps students become motivated to continue to keep up with related events.

Sports Maps

Take advantage of student interest in sports by developing map skills through locating major cities of various teams on a map.

Take a Stand

Choose a controversial issue from text material that students are currently studying or select a topic in the news. Designate one area of the classroom as strongly opposed to and another area as strongly for the issue. Ask students to move to the area that represents their views. Discussion should center on why they feel as they do. Then scramble the groups so that they represent mixed opinions and students can exchange points of view.

Time Lines

Give students a time line spanning a certain period covered in their reading. When reading the material, students choose the most important events to place on the time line. The class should compare the events selected for the time line.

What If ...?

Play "What If" games that change the course of events!
- What if women did not have the right to vote?
- What if slaves had not been freed?
- What if George McGovern instead of Richard Nixon had won the 1972 election?
- What if there had been no Watergate?

Who's Who

Cut out pictures or photographs of important people students are studying or have studied in their social studies text. Select one student to go to the front of the classroom where you pin one of the pictures or photographs on his/her back. Allow the other students in the class to see the photograph so that they can give information about the prominent figure to the student at the front of the room. The student has five tries to guess the name of the person in the photograph.

SCIENCE

A Book About Experiments

Have students write up all their science experiments, then bind them into books to present to the librarian for carding and displaying in the school library. To add interest to their books, ask students to write about themselves and include a photograph along with their own biographical data. Watch this page become the favorite page in their books.

Capillary Action/Surface Adhesion

To illustrate capillary action/surface adhesion, use two waxed paper cups and a double strip of absorbent paper towels. Fill one cup half full of water. Mark the water level on the outside of the cup. Place the empty cup beside the first cup. Bend the paper towels into a horseshoe shape, and place a "leg" of the towels in each cup. Leave overnight. To stimulate students' thinking, ask them to account for any difference in water level. Ask them to describe the condition of the paper towel. Have them tell about the part the many paper fibers play in water movement.

Classification

Ask students to find pictures in old newspapers or magazines of living and nonliving things. Have them cut out the pictures, place them in the two groups, and then paste them in a folder according to the group. Students will enjoy sharing their folders with other members of the class.

Collecting and Studying Insects

Collect a cricket for classroom study and place it in a cricket cage in a sunny window. Ask students to count the number of chirps that the cricket makes in one minute. Then move the cricket cage to a cool shelf. Have students count the number of chirps in the new environment. To check the relationship between the number of chirps and the environmental temperature, count the number of chirps in one minute, divide by four, add forty, and the result should be the approximate temperature near the cricket. Students can make charts or graphs to report their findings.

Form Some Triads

Divide the class into groups of three or triads. Ask each triad to research a topic in science, obtain materials, perform an experiment for the class, and teach a minilesson on the concept to the class. Triads invite new friendships, break down barriers, and encourage learning.

Human Movement

Let the sports pages of the newspaper help motivate students to learn about human movement. Ask students to analyze the sports section and circle any phrases dealing with human movement.

It Can't Be Done

Ask student to find a comic strip in which the character is defying the laws of science. Is a person walking up a wall or are animals talking? Have students write a paragraph explaining why the comic character is doing the impossible.

The Law of Jaws

When students use their hands to imitate the action of their jaws or those of a dog, they are apt to make both hands move up and down. After this experiment, they may be surprised to learn that their hands do not show how jaws work.

Give a cracker to each student. Ask them to break the cracker in half and chew one half while resting their forehead against the edge of their desk. Ask: Is it easy or difficult to chew in this position. Is it natural for the jaws to move? When the first half is swallowed, ask students to chew the second half of the cracker, but this time resting their chin on their desk. Ask: Is it easy or difficult to chew now? When the lower jaw cannot move, what must the head do to chew?

Ask students to observe other vertebrates—dogs, cats, horses, cows, fish, turtles, birds. In all these animals, ask students to observe which jaw moves in chewing—the upper, the lower, or both? Visit the zoo to observe an alligator and a snake feeding. Ask: Do their jaws work in the same way that humans' do?

Ask students to bring in a grasshopper or a beetle, two chewing insects, and look carefully through a magnifier at the insect's jaws. In what ways are they similar to ours? In what ways are they different?

Let Your Fingers Do the Shopping

Ask students to look through the newspaper for grocery store ads. Have them select advertised foods that they enjoy most and plan three nutritionally balanced meals from the foods advertised. Ask students to share their selections with a partner. Students enjoy cutting out the ads and pasting each of their meals on a round piece of paper that serves as a plate!

Wet and Wetter Water

This experiment requires two paper cups, detergent, two small cotton balls about the size of a large pea, and a half-inch length of yarn or string. Fill both cups with water and label them "A" and "B." Into cup "A," mix a little detergent. (Do not stir up suds.) Drop a cotton ball or string into cup "A" and cup "B" at the same time. To stimulate students' thinking, ask what happened to the cotton balls? Was there any difference in the wetting time between "A" and "B"? Why are detergents added to the family laundry? Can water be made "wetter" than "wet"?

What's the Weather?

Ask students to write daily weather reports in newspaper style.

MATHEMATICS

Counting Coins

When children are having difficulty counting groups of coins, provide a desk-size chart with the numbers 0–100 written in order. The child begins by figuring out the amount of the first coin and then putting a pencil on that amount on the chart. After looking at the next coin, the child figures out the amount and moves a pencil or finger the same number of spaces on the chart. The students continues until he/she has completed each money group problem.

"Draw" to Add, Subtract, or Multiply

This game can be played with two people, a small group, or

teams. One person is in charge of the cards, each of which has a number. Two cards are drawn and these two numbers are added, subtracted, or multiplied, depending on the level and the facts to be practiced. The arithmetic can be done orally, on paper, or on the chalkboard. Numbers of two or more digits can be made by drawing more cards. The winning individual or team receives a prize. Students enjoy this game because they can make up their own problems. They know it is fair because it is all in the luck of the draw.

Fraction Bump

Use a game board like a bingo card for this game. Make the board from a large index card that has been laminated. The board should have four blocks across and four rows of blocks. Write a fraction in each block. (Each fraction should be used twice). Chips or buttons of two different colors are needed as well as pictures of fractions on cards to match those on the game board. (Four or five pictures of each fraction are desirable). Two to six students take turns drawing a card, naming the fraction, and placing a chip on that fraction on the game board. If a player draws a fraction that is covered by a chip, the first player can be bumped off. The second player then places a chip on the fraction. To win, a player must cover four blocks in a vertical, horizontal, or diagonal line.

Go Fishing

This activity reinforces the skill of reducing fractions to their simplest form. It is adaptable to most math skills.

Teacher Directions: Make a fishing pole by tying a piece of yarn to a yardstick and attaching a magnet to the end of the line. Fold a piece of construction paper and cut out a small fish on the fold. On the outside of the fish, write a fraction that can be reduced. Open the fish and write the simplest form of the fraction inside. Put a paper clip on each fish.

Student Directions: Catch one fish and say the fraction in its simplest form, *aloud.* Open the fish to check your answer. If your answer is correct, keep the fish. If your answer is not correct, throw the fish back. The player with the most fish wins.

Jump to Add and Subtract

Use a sheet of butcher paper to make a life-size number line. Have individual students demonstrate how to add or subtract by jumping forward or backward on the number line. (Students love to take off their shoes to do this.) Teachers can read the number sentences from flash cards or they can make them up as they go. The problem can also be demonstrated on the overhead projector.

Math Motivator

For students who might be overwhelmed by an entire page of math problems, try this activity. Fold the page like an accordion and have students work one column at a time or instruct them to do all the problems containing a 2 first, then those containing a 3, etc.

Math Sponge

Write two digits on the board before students come to class. The assignment is to "Do all you can with those two digits." This activity encourages creativity while providing a review of basic math skills.

Measuring with Paper Clips

In discusssing measurement with students, make the point that the standard units of measurement are arbitrary and that others could be accepted and used. Suggest that students use paper clips as units of measurement in this activity. Ask them to hook 10 paper clips together and call this unit of length a "decaclip." By using a decaclip students can quickly find the length of an object that is 10 paper clips long. Using decaclips and single paper clips, ask them to measure the length of a table in paper clips. Then measure the width of the table in paper clips. Then point out that they can find the area of the table top in "square paper clips" by multiplying length times width.

Extend the activity by having students use common objects or containers as standard units in the measurement of weight and volume. For example, they can use steel washers and nails as units of weight, and juice cans as units of volume.

Metric Conversion

To give students an extra hook to aid in seeing and remembering the process of metric conversion, teach them the mnemonic "King Hector Died Spacey Drinking Chocolate Milk." Now draw a staircase with the king on the top step and each word of the sentence in order on a descending step. The step "Space" must be counted. It stands for the basic unit—that is, meter, liter, or gram. For example:

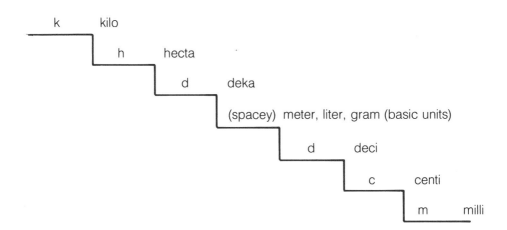

To convert from one unit of measure to another—to go up the stairs, move the decimal point to the left; to go down the stairs, move the decimal point to the right. For example, 3 m = 3000 mm; 65 cm = .00065 km; 4 ml = .0041; and 7.6 g = 760 cg.

Number Recognition

Play Bingo to reinforce number recognition from 1 to 99.

Place Value/Trading/Renaming

This activity requires between 500 and 1,000 drinking straws or popsicle sticks and some rubber bands. Toss the straws or popsicle sticks in the middle of the floor in the classroom and ask students to tell how many there are. They quickly see how difficult it is to count them. At that point, begin grouping the straws or sticks in tens, hundreds, and ones. Students who have had a hard time grasping the idea of trading and bundling when the ones place has more that ten straws will begin to understand the concept. With the straws or sticks bundled in hundreds, tens, and ones, throw them out on the floor again so that students can see how easy it is to count the bundles. When the subject of renaming comes up in subtraction, the student can subtract or give the teacher a number only if the tens bundle can be renamed as ten ones.

Play Cards

This classwide activity reinforces place value concepts through hundreds (or higher if appropriate for your students). Prepare cards like a deck of playing cards and number them from one to ninety-nine. Shuffle the deck and give one card to each student until every card is dealt. Some students will have several depending on the size of the class. One person starts by reading the number on his/her card. The person who has the answer, gives it and then reads his/her question. Play continues until the original number is repeated. For example, (1) My number is 10. Who has a number with a 3 in the ones place? (2) My number is 23. Who has a number with a 4 in the tens place and a 1 in the ones place? (3) My number is 41. Who has a number with a 1 in the hundreds place?

Practice Your Number Facts

Cut construction paper in whatever shapes the children like. Punch eight or nine holes along the perimeter of the shape. Write a number by each hole and a number in the middle of the shape with an addition, subtraction, multiplication, or division sign beside it. On the back of the shape beside each hole, write the answer to the number fact that results from combining the number in the center with the number beside the hole on the front. Have children say the number fact as they stick their pencil through a hole, turning the shape over to check the correct answer, which is on the back beside the pencil point.

Secret Code

To reinforce the learning of place value, have students play the secret code game. This activity is adaptable to most math skills.

Teacher Directions: Cut a manila folder in half. Cut out decimal numbers from an index card and glue them to the inside of the folder. For example: 3.332. Tape a sheet of paper over the numbers so that they become invisible. On the outside of the folder write the words for the numbers students are to learn. For example: Three and three hundred thirty-two thousandths.

Student Directions: Write the numbers for the words written on the front of each folder at the top of your scrap paper. Open the folder and make a rubbing (using your pencil and scrap paper) of the white sheet inside. As you rub, the correct answer will appear like magic! Check your work.

Spin the Math Bottle

Tape a number on a plastic soft drink bottle. Give each child a card containing a number. Spin the bottle. The child who is pointed to must multiply (or add) the number on the card by the number on the bottle.

Teacher, May I?

Divide the class into two to four teams. Using multiplication flash cards, call out a fact to the first student in Team I. If the correct answer is given, record the answer as the number of points earned (for example, for 7 x 6 = 42, Team I would get 42 points). Go to the first student in Team II. If the student gives the correct answer, award Team II the appropriate number of points. The first team to win 400 points wins the game.

Teaching Time

Here's a trick to help children tell the difference between the minute and the hour hand on a clock. Compare the words *minute* and *hour*. Minute is the longer word, and it is also the longer of the two hands.

Tens and Ones

Refer to the word TO to help children distinguish the digit in the tens place from the digit in the ones place. (Almost everyone can remember the word TO.)

ADAPTABLE TO ALL SUBJECTS

Basic Skill Flash Cards

Give each child two envelopes. Ask students to draw a rainbow on one and a rain cloud on the other. Have them put flash cards for the words they don't know in the envelope with the rain cloud and flash cards for the words they do know in the envelope with the rainbow. Then have each student select a partner with whom to study. As students learn new words they move the cards to the envelope with the rainbow. This game works equally well with number facts. Students will work hard to move their flash cards to the rainbow envelope.

Board Games

This activity is another timesaver for teachers. Prepare permanent boards for class games—ticktacktoe, concentration, athletic fields (baseball, basketball, or football), and open-ended track games. Laminate the boards. Make different sets of cards to use with the master boards for any subject area. The use of such games reinforces skills in an exciting way.

Calendar of Events

With the help of some of the new computer software, some teachers are giving their students a calendar of events for units in a variety of subject areas. This makes students and parents aware of the teacher's expectations. Test dates are announced early and students, with encouragement from parents, may begin preparation before the last minute.

Gimmicks

Students want a different approach when learning—especially low achievers. Ask a business to donate a time clock and have students clock in and out when they come to class. This is a great motivator and developer of practical math skills. For example, students can compute work time based on the current minimum wage. Also consider using a cash register, adding machine, typewriter, or old motor as a teaching device.

Jeopardy

Materials: Pocket with money amounts

Play money

Questions according to difficulty level on cards

Play this game in teams of four to five children. Each child takes a turn selecting a card, but the *team* can help with the question. In that way all members are learning! Use a timer to tell the teams when to stop and count the money they have won for their correct answers. The team with the most money wins. Young children love this game!

Magic Slates

Magic slates (available at variety stores) or individual chalkboards can be used as an excellent motivating device appropriate in kindergarten through graduate school. Students write answers to questions or problems on individual slates. When the teacher says, "Slates up," all students respond. This strategy gives teachers a one-on-one with every student. It lets them know whether to stay on the objective or move on if students have mastered material.

Memory King or Queen

After a lesson has been taught, later during the day orally quiz students on the material covered. The pupil who remembers most is the Memory King or Queen. (Younger students enjoy wearing a paper crown for the remainder of the school day.)

Mr. or Ms. Know-It-All

Select one person to go to the front of the classroom to become Mr. or Ms. Know-It-All. Other students then question their classmate about the day's assignment. When the student at the front is stumped, the person who asked the question becomes Mr. or Ms. Know-It-All, provided that student can give the correct answer to the question just asked.

Pathfinder

While the use of a pathfinder, a step-by-step instructional tool that introduces a library user to the variety of information available, helps all students develop better library skills, it is especially valuable for the low achiever. A pathfinder offers the student a roadmap to use in writing a report, a speech, a book. Pathfinders are based on the materials available in the school library. They might include reference sources, relevant periodicals, periodical indexes, selected call numbers to use in browsing, subject headings in the card catalog, subject headings for periodicals, nonprint media, and related fiction. Pathfinders are developed on one specific topic and may be used in all subject areas.

Pick a Clothespin

To teach any skill or concept involving a one- or two-word answer, use a cardboard wheel (some pizza shops are willing to give teachers a few of their boards) on which you have written a series of questions, statements, or words in an area the size of a piece of pie. Write the one- or two-word answer on wooden clothespins. Students take turns drawing a clothespin and matching the answer to the corresponding question on the cardboard wheel. This activity is appropriate for a group, for one or two students, or for an individual. Wheels, clothespins, and cans for storing clothespins may be color-coded for use with young children.

Second Chance

Instead of writing the basic skill objectives and accompanying activities for each day on the chalkboard, develop a chart system. Even though initially this will take a great deal of time to develop, it is cost effective because charts can be laminated and used repeatedly. This technique allows for mobility of the student's work and will help the child who needs more time or practice because work is not erased at the end of the day.

Secret Object

A student picks an object in the classroom and tells the teacher what it is. Classmates ask questions to guess the secret object. Only questions with yes and no answers are allowed. If the questioner gets a yes answer, she or he continues questioning. If a no answer is given, another student asks a question. This is a good opportunity for students to improve their skill in using such terms as north, south, east, west, round, square, rectangle, cube, opposite, same, similar to, above, beyond, beside, near.

Semantic Mapping

Choose a word central to the topic being studied and write it on the chalkboard. Ask the class to brainstorm words related to the keyword. Categorize the words given. Now have a discussion on those words. This strategy may be used for general vocabulary development; it also helps students relate new material to prior knowledge. It is an effective culminating activity to help students visually see how much knowledge they have gained.

Subject Folders

Make a folder for each student for each subject. As students complete their work, they *immediately* place it in the appropriate folder. This strategy helps the teacher as well as the low-achieving student get organized.

Who Works in the Funnies?

Have students read all the comics in one day's newspaper. Ask them to make a list of the jobs that the comic strip characters hold. Then have them write a brief description of the duties for each job. Allow them to share their work with the class.

Wisdom Wheel

At the end of each day have children tell three or four facts they have learned during the day. List the facts on the board and leave them there until the following afternoon. Then transfer the facts in question form to cards. The cards should be color-coded—for example, purple for social studies, green for science, orange for math, and blue for vocabulary. Make a wheel, dividing it into the same color categories as the cards. After two or three weeks there will be enough question cards to begin the game. Three or four students play at a time, taking turns spinning the wheel and answering a question from the color category where the wheel stops. For each correct answer, the student earns a check on a game card. Students do not compete with one another; they earn checks for themselves, up to four checks each day. When they acquire twenty-five checks, students may receive a reward—for example, a pass to the game center or a free reading period. This game is fun for children to play. Since they contribute to making up the questions, they can experience success while reinforcing learning.

MOTIVATION / SELF-CONCEPT

Class Brag Book

To brag is to praise one's own qualities or accomplishments. Make a scrapbook recognizing students in the class for achievements. All students contribute because all have things to brag about. Display the brag book in a prominent place in the classroom.

Dial-a-Parent

Each week call a parent with some honest and positive report about his or her child. If the parent does not have a telephone, a postcard with the same report will work as well.

Good News

Designate a few minutes each day for Good News time. Allow students to share something good that has happened to them since the last time they shared Good News. Teachers should also tell something from time to time. Everyone will not participate every day, but teachers who forget about Good News will be reminded by the student who has something to tell. Students will begin showing more interest in one another. And low achievers will realize that there are positive things to say about themselves.

Home Run

This activity will appeal to the sports-minded student while encouraging good behavior. Draw a baseball diamond on poster board and laminate it. Cut out a baseball player and place a piece of magnetic tape on each base of the diamond and on the back of the player. Move the player to a base to reward the class for something it has done well. When the player reaches home plate, reward the class with ten extra minutes of free time or some other appropriate reward.

A Jar Full of Corn

Reward the class for good control of noise, talking, etc., by transferring a spoonful of popcorn from a larger jar to a smaller jar. Look for good behavior when students are lining up for recess, during lunch, or during transition times. For noisy behavior, remove a spoonful of popcorn from the smaller jar and return it to the larger one. When the smaller jar is filled, reward the class with a popcorn party.

Make an "I Can" Can

Cover a small fruit juice can with bright contact paper. Paste a picture of an eye cut from a magazine on the outside of the can. When a student says, "I can't," give her or him an *I Can*. This may be a goldfish cracker, a pencil, a pass to go to the listening center, or whatever the teacher wishes to keep in the *I Can*. The purpose is to encourage students to engage in positive self-talk.

Name Tags

Write each child's name on a tag with a hook attached. On entering the classroom each morning, each child removes his/her name tag, hanging on the door or the chalk tray, and places it in a basket. Since the names in the basket represent those present each day, the teacher can draw tags from it to determine who will answer special questions or to decide who will be the leader for the day. Students like to "be drawn from the basket."

The Nicest Thing Ever

Make a "Nicest-Thing-Ever" book by asking students to write and/or illustrate (a) The Nicest Thing I Ever Did for Anyone (ask them to explain what it was, why they did it, and how it made them feel); (b) The Nicest Thing Anyone Ever Did for Me (ask them to describe it, why they think someone did it, and how it made a difference in what might have happened); (c) The Nicest Thing I Ever Did for Myself.

Nontouching Hugs

There are some positive thinkers who say that "everyone needs six hugs a day: three to feel good about themselves and three to give away." Discuss the meaning of a hug with students. Talk about how hugs make people feel. Make sure students realize that a hug does not require touching. Then think of as many ways as possible to let students know you care about them. For example, wink at a child and tell him/her that it was a hug. Design your own note pad—"Hugs from the desk of _____." Use stickers with hug themes. Bring in a "hug jar" containing candy. Give coupons redeemable for a hug at home. Read "hug" books. Smile genuinely and often.

Off to a Good Start

Before school begins, upon receipt of the class roster, send a postcard to each incoming student. A brief note letting all students know that their teacher is looking forward to the pleasure of their company is a fine way to start the school year.

Positive Strokes

Write each student's name on a piece of paper and place it in a basket. Students draw a name and write a descriptive paragraph, using only positive statements, about that person. Students read their paragraphs to the class and classmates guess the name of the person described. All students enjoy hearing nice things being said about them.

Reading Buddies

Allow two students to sit together and read, using games or flashcards from a "Buddy Box." Children especially enjoy reading stories to each other and planning "concentration" with reading flashcards.

Self-Concept Bingo

Prepare bingo cards with blank spaces (no numbers) for the names of every student in the class. Give each student a copy of the blank card. Have an autograph party for *every* class member to sign in one of the blocks on each card. Now, every student has a bingo card with the names of peers in place of numbers. Put all students' names on separate slips of paper in a box and draw one name at a time. Proceed as if playing bingo.

Something to Roar About

Assign each student one "display station" consisting of a sheet of construction paper labeled with the students' name. Use the display station to show the student's work. This can consist of the best work the student has completed during the week or something from a subject area in which the student has shown improvement. Students may change their display whenever they like.

Sticker Fun

Put seasonal stickers on papers to encourage younger students to work hard for the next appropriate sticker. Who wants a Halloween sticker with Thanksgiving coming? Students will begin taking more pride in their work. The work of the low achiever, which is sometimes ignored, will also be on display.

Student of the Week

On Friday draw a student's name to be "Student of the Week" for the following week. Send home a "good news" note to the parents to explain what is involved and suggest that they take part in planning the student's presentation to the class. On Monday after a private meeting with the teacher, the student tells the class about her/himself. The presentation may include photos, trophies, or other significant items. Other students listen, ask questions, and write a story about the Student of the Week. Class members then shares their stories, thus giving everyone an opportunity to say something nice about the student being honored. Display the stories on the bulletin board, along with a picture of the student and a large gold star designating the student of the week. Notify former teachers of the student so that they can congratulate her or him and reinforce good feelings and positive behavior. The student also has responsibility for being line leader, monitor, messenger, and teacher assistant for proofreading the stories written by the class. At the end of the week, the student draws the name of a successor. The stories are taken down from the bulletin board and stapled inside a construction paper folder, along with the picture, the star, the student's name, and the date. With the special attention and recognition, the student of the week becomes a model student worthy of the title.

Success/Failure

To help students gain self-confidence and overcome the fear of failure, read descriptions of "important people" and ask the following question: Based only on the information presented, do you think this person was a success or failure in life? Then ask students to guess the name of the person you described. Examples might include—

- He ran for political office seven times and was defeated each time. (Abraham Lincoln)
- In sports, he struck out 1,330 times. (Babe Ruth)
- In trying to solve a problem, she tried 487 experiments all of which failed. (Madam Curie)

Have students develop their own success/failure descriptions of people they admire.

Success Sheet

In some classes teachers need to structure ways students can affirm themselves on a daily basis. One strategy is to use a success sheet for students who begin each day or class period by completing a positive statement about themselves. For example,

Monday—I am a person of great value. Today I _____.

Tuesday—I am glad I am me. Today I _____.

Wednesday—I am special; there is no one else in the world just like me. Today I _____.

Thursday—I am proud of myself. Today I _____.

Friday—I am a good person. I like myself. Today I _____.

A student who is a low achiever or who has a poor self-image may need help at first identifying successful behaviors and efforts. On Friday, after completing the daily statement, students and teacher form a circle and each student tells the class about one success from those listed for the week. This time may be used to help students understand the importance of listening and showing respect for peers, knowing that it will be important to have classmates reciprocate. Students keep all their sheets in individual success folders that are reviewed from time to time by students and teacher.

A Teacher You Will Be

When a student has mastered a concept or skill, allow her/him to teach it to a group of peers. To make the student feel important, give her/him a special "teacherette badge" to wear while teaching. The topic need not be a school subject; the student could share a special talent with peers.

Teddy Bear Day

Ask each child to bring a favorite teddy bear, doll, or other stuffed animal from home on a particular day. Have all the animals wear name tags with stickers matching the student's name tag. All students tell what is special about their animals. Participation is success on teddy bear day.

Time Off

Give students who complete assigned classwork during the alloted time 15 or 20 minutes of free time on Friday as a reward for their hard work and good behavior. Students who do not complete their work use this time to complete assignments.

What's Right

Check all the correct items on students' papers. Encourage students to take these papers home to be signed by Mom and/or Dad.

BIBLIOGRAPHY

1. Achilles, C. M. "A Vision of Better Schools." In *Instructional Leadership*, edited by William Greenfield. Newton, Mass.: Allyn and Bacon, 1987.
2. Anderson, L. "The Environment of Instruction: The Function of Seatwork in a Commercially Developed Curriculum." In *Comprehensive Instruction: Perspectives and Suggestions*, edited by G. Duffy, L. Roehler, and J. Mason. New York: Longman, 1984.
3. Andrews, Richard L., and Soder, Roger. "Principal Leadership and Student Achievement." *Educational Leadership* 44, no. 66 (March 1987): 9–11.
4. Apple, Michael W. "Curriculum in the Year 2000." *Phi Delta Kappan* 64, no. 1 (January 1983): 321–26.
5. Aspy, David, and Roebuck, Flora N. *Kids Don't Learn from People They Don't Like*. Amherst, Mass.: Human Resource Development Press, 1977.
6. Ausubel, David. *The Psychology of Meaningful Verbal Learning*. New York: Grune and Stratton, 1963.
7. _____. "In Defense of Advance Organizers: A Reply to the Critics." *Review of Educational Research* 48, no. 2 (1978): 251–57.
8. Bang-Jensen, Valerie. "The View from Next Door: A Look at Peer 'Supervision'." In *Improving Teaching*, edited by Karen K. Zumwalt. Alexandria, Va.: Association for Supervision and Curriculum Development, 1986.
9. Banks, James A., with Clegg, Ambrose A., Jr. *Teaching Strategies for the Social Studies: Inquiry, Valuing, and Decision-making*. Reading, Mass: Addison-Wesley Publishing Co., 1973.
10. Barth, Roland. *Education Week,* May 9, 1984.
11. Becker, Henry Jan, and Epstein, Joyce L. "Parent Involvement: A Survey of Teacher Practices." *Elementary School Journal* 83, no. 2 (November 1982): 85–102.
12. Bloom, B. S. *Human Characteristics and Student Learning*. New York: McGraw-Hill, 1976.
13. Bossert, S. "Effective Elementary Schools." In *Reading for Excellence: An Effective Schools Sourcebook*, edited by R. Kyle. Washington, D.C.: U. S. Government Printing Office, 1985.
14. Boyer, Ernest L. "Early Schooling and the Nation's Future." *Educational Leadership* 44, no. 6 (March 1987): 4–8.
15. _____. *High School: A Report on Secondary Education in America*. New York: Harper Colophon Books, Harper and Row Publishers, 1983.

16. Bracht, G. H., and Hopkins, K. D. "Stability of Educational Achievement." In *Perspectives in Educational and Psychological Measurement,* edited by G. H. Bracht, K. D. Hopkins, and J. C. Stanley. Englewood Cliffs, N. J.: Prentice-Hall, 1972.
17. Brandt, Ronald S., ed. *Educational Leadership* 44, no. 6 (March 1987). (This entire issue is devoted to at-risk students.)
18. Bronfenbrenner, Urie. "Alienation and the Four Worlds of Childhood." *Phi Delta Kappan* 67 (February 1986): 430–36.
19. Brookover, W., and others. *Creating Effective Schools.* Holmes Beach, Fla.: Learning Publications, 1987.
20. Brophy, Jere E. "Synthesis of Research on Strategies for Motivating Students to Learn." *Educational Leadership* 45, no. 2 (October 1987): 40–48.
21. Brophy, Jere E., and Evertson, Carolyn M. *Learning from Teaching: A Developmental Perspective.* Boston: Allyn and Bacon, 1976.
22. Brophy, Jere, E., and Good, Thomas L. *Teacher-Student Relationships: Causes and Consequences.* New York: Holt, Rinehart and Winston, 1974.
23. _____. "Teacher Effects." In *Third Handbook of Research on Teaching,* edited by M. Wittrock. New York: Macmillan, 1985.
24. Burkle, Candace Regan, and Marshak, David. *Study Skills Program,* Level 1. Reston, Va.: National Association of Secondary School Principals, 1980.
25. Canfield, Jack, and Wells, Harold C. *100 Ways to Enhance Self-Concept in the Classroom.* New York: Prentice-Hall, 1976.
26. Canter, Lee. *Assertive Discipline.* Santa Monica, Calif.: Canter and Associates, 1976.
27. Carbo, Marie. "Matching Reading Styles: Correcting Ineffective Instruction." *Educational Leadership* 45, no. 2 (October 1987): 55–57.
28. Carbo, Marie; Dunn, Rita; and Dunn, Kenneth. *Teaching Students to Read Through Their Individual Learning Styles.* Englewood Cliffs, N. J.: Prentice Hall, 1986.
29. Clark, R. "Reconsidering Research on Learning from Media." *Review of Educational Research* 53, no. 4 (1983): 445–59.
30. Clauset, Karl H., Jr., and Gaynor, Alan K. "Improving Schools for Low-Achieving Children: A System Dynamics Policy Study." Paper preesented at the Annual Meeting of the American Educational Research Association, New York, 1982. ED 214 243
31. Cloer, Thomas. *A Teacher's Handbook of Language Experience Activities.* Greenville, S.C.: Furman Press, 1987.
32. Collins, Marva, and Tamarkin, Civia. *Marva Collins' Way.* Los Angeles: Jeremy P. Tarcher, 1982.

33. Comer, James. "New Haven's School-Community Connection." *Educational Leadership* 44, no. 6 (March 1987): 13–16.
34. Corcoran, T. "Effective Secondary Schools." In *Reaching for Excellence: An Effective Schools Sourcebook,* edited by R. Kyle. Washington, D.C.: U.S. Government Printing Office, 1985.
35. Costa, Arthur L. *Developing Minds: A Resource Book for Teaching Thinking.* Alexandria, Va.: Association for Supervision and Curriculum Development, 1985.
36. Csikszentmihalyi, Mihaly, and McCormack, Jane. "The Influence of Teachers." *Phi Delta Kappan* 67, no. 6 (February 1986): 415–19.
37. Cummins, Jim. "Empowering Minority Students: A Framework for Intervention." *Harvard Educational Review* 56, no. 1 (February 1986): 18–36.
38. deBono, Edward. *CORT Program.* Elmsford, N.Y.: Pergamon Press, 1986.
39. Dishon, Dee, and O'Leary, Pat Wilson. *A Guidebook for Cooperative Learning: A Technique for Creating More Effective Schools.* Holmes Beach, Fla.: Learning Publications, 1984.
40. Dorman, Gayle. *Improving Middle-Grade Schools.* Chapel Hill, N.C.: Center for Early Adolescence, 1987.
41. Doyle, W. "Effective Secondary School Practices." In *Reaching for Excellence: An Effective Schools Sourcebook,* edited by R. Kyle. Washington, D.C.: U.S. Government Printing Office, 1985.
42. Edmonds, R. R. "Some Schools Work and More Can." Social Policy 9 (March/April 1979): 28–32.
43. *Effective Teaching: Observations from Research.* Arlington, Va.: American Association of School Administrators, 1986.
44. Evertson, Carolyn M. "Differences in Instructional Activities in Higher and Lower Achieving Junior High English and Math Classes." *Elementary School Journal* 82, no. 4 (March 1982): 329–50.
45. Feldman, Ruth Duskin. "What Are Thinking Skills? These Ideas Can Help You Cultivate a Thoughtful Classroom." *Instructor* 95 (April 1986): 34–39.
46. Felker, D. *Building Positive Self-Concepts.* Minneapolis: Burgess, 1974.
47. Finn, C. E., Jr. "Toward Strategic Independence: Nine Commandments for Enhancing School Effectiveness." *Phi Delta Kappan* 65, no. 8 (April 1984): 513–24.
48. Frechtling, Joy, and others. *A Review of Programs and Strategies Used in Other American School Systems for Improving Student Achievement.* Rockville, Md.: Montgomery County Public Schools, Department of Educational Accountability, 1984. ED 255 584

49. Frymier, Jack. *Motivation to Learn.* West Lafayette, Ind.: Kappa Delta Pi, 1985.

50. Fuchs, Lynn S., and others. *A Comparison of Mastery Learning Procedures Among High and Low Ability Students,* 1985. ED 259 307

51. Ginsburg, A., and Hanson, S. *Values and Educational Success Among Disadvantaged Students.* Washington, D.C.: U.S. Department of Education, 1985.

52. Glasser, William. "Self-Importance Boosts Learning." *School Administrator* 45, no. 1 (January 1988): 16–17.

53. Good Thomas L. "Teacher Expectations and Student Perceptions: A Decade of Research." *Educational Leadership* 38, no. 5 (February 1981): 415–22.

54. Good, Thomas L., and Stipek, D. "Individual Differences in the Classroom: A Psychological Perspective." In *National Study of School Evaluation Yearbook,* edited by G. Fenstermacher and J. Goodlad. Chicago: University of Chicago Press, 1983.

55. Good, Thomas L., and Brophy, Jere E. *Looking in Classrooms.* New York: Harper and Row, 1984.

56. _____. *Educational Psychology.* 3d ed. White Plains, N.Y.: Longman, 1986.

57. Goodlad, John I. *A Place Called School.* New York: McGraw-Hill, 1984.

58. _____. "Curriculum and Effective Teaching." In *Perspectives on Effective Teaching and the Cooperative Classroom,* edited by Judy Reinhartz. Washington, D.C.: National Education Association, 1984.

59. Gordon, Ira J. *Research Report of Parent-Oriented Home-Based Early Childhood Education Programs.* Gainesville, Fla.: Institute for Development of Human Resources, University of Florida, 1975.

60. Graves, Donald H. *Writing: Teachers and Children at Work.* Portsmouth, N.H.: Heinemann Educational Books, 1983.

61. Greene, Lawrence J. *Kids Who Underachieve.* New York: Simon and Schuster, 1986.

62. Hanley, Patricia E., and Swick, Kevin J. *Teacher Renewal: Revitalization of Classroom Teachers.* Washington, D.C.: National Education Association, 1983.

63. Heath, Douglas H. "Developing Teachers Not Just Techniques" In *Improving Teaching,* edited by Karen K. Zumwalt. Alexandria, Va.: Association for Supervision and Curriculum Development, 1986.

64. Heitzmann, William Ray. *Educational Games and Simulations.* Rev. ed. Washington, D.C.: National Education Association, 1983.

65. _____. *The Newspaper in the Classroom.* 2d ed. Washington,

D. C.: National Education Association, 1986.

66. Heller, Harold W.; Spooner, Fred; Anderson, Dana M.; and Mims, Aquilla A. "Homework: A Review of Special Education Classroom Practices in the Southeast." Accepted for publication in *Teacher Education* and *Special Education*.

67. Hobbs, N., ed. *The Futures of Children: Categories, Labels, and Their Consequences*. Nashville, Tenn.: Vanderbilt University Press, 1975.

68. Hornbeck, David W. "Technology and Students at Risk." In *Proceedings of the Conference on Technology and Students at Risk of School Failure*, June 1987. Sponsored by Agency for Instructional Technology, Box 8, Bloomington, IN 47402-0120.

69. Hosford, Philip L., ed. *Using What We Know About Teaching*. Alexandria, Va.: Association for Supervision and Curriculum Development, 1984.

70. Hunter, Madeline. *Improved Instruction*. El Segundo, Calif.: TIP Publications, 1985.

71. Hunter, Madeline, and Baker, George. "If at First ... Attribution Theory in the Classroom." *Educational Leadership* 45, no. 2 (October 1987): 50–54.

72. Johnson, D. *The Social Psychology of Education*. New York: Holt, Rinehart and Winston, 1970.

73. Johnson, D. W., and Johnson, R. T. *Learning Together and Alone*. 2d ed. Englewood Cliffs, N. J.: Prentice Hall, 1986.

74. Johnson, D. W.; Johnson, R. T.; and Holubec, E. *Circles of Learning: Cooperation in the Classroom*. Rev. ed. Edina, Minn: Interaction Book Co., 1986.

75. Johnson, David W., and Johnson, Frank P. *Joining Together*. 3d ed. Englewood Cliffs, N.J.: Prentice Hall, 1987.

76. Johnson, David W., and Johnson, Roger T. "Research Shows the Benefits of Adult Cooperation." *Educational Leadership* 44, no. 6 (March 1987): 27–30.

77. Johnson, Kenneth. "Culturally Disadvantaged." *Journal of Secondary Education* 45, no. 1 (January 1970): 43–47.

78. Jones, Beau Fly. "Quality and Equality Through Cognitive Instruction." *Educational Leadership* 44, no. 7 (April 1986): 5–11.

79. Jones, Beau Fly, and others, eds. *Strategic Teaching and Learning: Cognitive Instruction in the Content Areas*. Alexandria, Va.: Association for Supervision and Curriculum Development, 1987.

80. Jones, Vernon F., and Jones, Louise S. *Comprehensive Classroom Management: Creating Positive Learning Environments*. 2d ed. Boston: Allyn and Bacon, 1986.

81. Joyce, Bruce; Showers, Beverly; and Rolheiser-Bennett, Carol.

"Staff Development and Student Learning: A Synthesis of Research on Models of Teaching." *Educational Leadership* 45, no. 2 (October 1987): 11–23.

82. Kepner, Henry S., Jr., ed. *Computers in the Classroom*. 2d ed. Washington, D.C.: National Education Association, 1986.

83. Kerman, Sam. "A Grassroots Project: Teaching Expectations and Student Achievement." *Phi Delta Kappan* 60, no. 10 (June 1979): 717–18.

84. LaConte, Ronald T., and Doyle, Mary Anne. *Homework as a Learning Experience*. 2d ed. Washington, D.C.: National Education Association, 1986.

85. Lehr, Judy B. *A Final Report of the Furman University Center of Excellence*. Greenville, S.C.: Furman Press, 1987.

86. Levin, Henry M. "Accelerated Schools for Disadvantaged Students." *Educational Leadership* 44, no. 6 (March 1987): 19–21.

87. Levin, Tamar, and others. "Behavioral Patterns of Students Under an Individualized Learning Strategy." *Instructional Science* 9 (1980): 85–100.

88. Levin, Tamar, with Long, Ruth. *Effective Instruction*. Alexandria, Va.: Association for Supervision and Curriculum Development, 1981, p. 7.

89. Lindgren, S. E., and Richman, L. C. "Immediate Memory Functions of Verbally Deficient Reading-Disabled Children." *Journal of Learning Disabilities* 17, no. 4 (April 1984): 222–25

90. Lipsitz, Joan. *Successful Schools for Young Adolescents*. New Brunswick, N. J.: Transaction Books, 1984.

91. Lock, Corey. *Study Skills*. West Lafayette, Ind.: Kappa Delta Pi, 1981.

92. Lortie, Dan. *School Teacher*. Chicago: University of Chicago Press, 1975.

93. McGinnis, Ellen, and Goldstein, Arnold P. *Skill-Streaming the Elementary School Child*. Champaign, Ill.: Research Press Co., 1984.

94. Martin, William R. "Teacher Behaviors—Do They Make a Difference? A Review of the Research." *Kappa Delta Pi Record* (December 1979): 48–50.

95. Metz, Mary H. *Classrooms and Corridors: The Crisis of Authority in Desegregated Schools*. Los Angeles: University of California Press, 1978.

96. _____. "Sources of Constructive Social Relationships in an Urban Magnet School." *American Journal of Education* 91, no. 2 (February 1983): 202–45.

97. Mitchell, William, and Conn, Charles Paul. *The Power of Positive Students*. New York: Bantam Books, 1985.

98. Moffett, Kenneth J., and Clisby, Mara. "Share the Adventure of Peer Coaching." *School Administrator* 45, no. 1 (January 1988): 14–15.

99. Moorman, Chick; Dishon, Dee; and O'Leary, Pat Wilson. "Overview of Cooperative Learning: A Strategy for Effective Teaching." In *Perspectives on Effective Teaching and the Cooperative Classroom,* edited by Judy Reinhartz. Washington, D.C.: National Education Association, 1984.

100. Murphy, Joseph; Hallinger, Philip; and Lotto, Linda. "Inequitable Allocations of Alterable Learning Variables." *Journal of Teacher Education* 37, no. 6 (November-December 1986): 21–26.

101. National Foundation for the Improvement of Education. *Operation Rescue: A Blueprint for Success.* Washington, D.C.: NFIE, 1986.

102. _____.*Community Mobilization for Dropout Prevention: A Blueprint for Success.* Washington, D.C.: NFIE, 1987.

103. Oakes, Jeannie. "Keeping Track, Part I: The Policy and Practice of Curriculum Inequality." *Phi Delta Kappan* 68 (September 1986): 12–17.

104. Ohanian, Susan. "Question of the Day." *English Journal* 72, no. 7 (November 1983): 37–43.

105. Pellicano, Roy R. "At Risk: A View of 'Social Advantage'." *Educational Leadership* 44, no. 6 (March 1987): 47–49.

106. Peterson, Penelope L.; Janicki, Terence C.; and Swing, Susan R. "Ability x Treatment Interaction Effects on Children's Learning in Large-Group and Small-Group Approaches." *American Educational Research Journal* 18, no. 4 (Winter 1981): 453-73.

107. Pressley, Michael; Levin, Joel; and Delaney, H. "The Mnemonic Keyword Method." *Review of Educational Research* 52, no. 1 (January 1982): 61–91.

108. Purkey, S. C., and Smith, M. S. "Effective Schools: A Review." *Elementary School Journal* 83, no. 4 (March 1983): 427–52.

109. Purkey, W. W., and Novak, J. *Inviting School Success.* 2d ed. Belmont, Calif: Wadsworth Publishing Co., 1984.

110. Purkey, William W. *Self-Concept and School Achievement.* Englewood Cliffs, N. J.: Prentice-Hall, 1970.

111. Purkey, William W., and Schmidt, John J. *The Inviting Relationship.* Englewood Cliffs, N.J.: Prentice-Hall, 1987.

112. Purkey, Willliam W., and Strahan, David B. *Positive Discipline: A Pocketful of Ideas.* Columbus, Ohio: National Middle School Association, 1986.

113. Redfield, D. L., and Rousseau, E. W. "A Meta-Analysis of Experimental Research on Teaching Questioning Behavior." *Review of Educational Research* 51, no. 4 (1981): 237–45.

114. Reinhartz, Judy, and Reinhartz, Dennis. *Teach-Practice-Apply: The TPA Instruction Model,* 7–12. Washington, D.C.: National Education Association, 1988.

115. Reinhartz, Judy, and Van Cleaf, David. *Teach-Practice Apply: The TPA Instruction Model,* K–8. Washington, D.C.: National Education Association, 1986.

116. *Report of the Dropout Prevention Task Force,* Nikki Setzler, Chairman. Columbia, S.C.: South Carolina Department of Education, 1987.

117. Restak, Richard. *The Brain: The Last Frontier.* Garden City, N.Y.: Doubleday and Co., 1979.

118. Rich, Dorothy. *Schools and Families: Issues and Actions.* Washington, D.C.: National Education Association, 1987.

119. _____. *Teachers and Parents: An Adult-to-Adult Approach.* Washington, D.C.: National Education Association, 1987.

120. Rimm, Sylvia B. "How to Reach the Underachiever." *Instructor* 94 (September 1985): 72–76.

121. Rowe, Mary Budd. "Wait-Time and Rewards as Instructional Variables, Their Influence on Language, Logic and Fate Control: Part I, Wait-Time." *Journal of Research in Science Teaching* 11, no. 2 (1974): 81–94.

122. Salomone, Ronald E., ed. *Teaching the Low-Level Achiever.* Chillicothe, Ohio: Division of Humanities, Ohio University, 1986. ED 270 789

123. Sharp, Billy B., with Weldon, Ward. *Learning: The Rhythm of Risk.* Rosemont, Ill.: Combined Motivation Education Systems, 1971.

124. Silvernail, David L. *Teaching Styles as Related to Student Achievement.* 2d ed. Washington, D.C.: National Education Association, 1986.

125. Slavin, Robert E. *Cooperative Learning.* New York: Longman, 1983.

126. _____. *Using Student Team Learning.* 3d ed. Baltimore, Md.: Johns Hopkins University, 1986.

127. _____. "Cooperative Learning and the Cooperative School." *Educational Leadership* 45, no. 3 (November 1987): 7–13.

128. _____. *Cooperative Learning: Student Teams.* 2d ed. Washington, D.C.: National Education Association, 1987.

129. _____. "Cooperative Revolution Catches Fire." *School Administrator* 45, no. 1 (January 1988): 9–13.

130. Smith, C. R. *Learning Disabilities: Interaction of Learner, Task and Setting.* Boston: Little Brown and Co., 1983.

131. Squires, David A.: Huitt, William G.: and Segard, John K. *Effec-*

tive Schools and Classrooms: A Research-Based Perspective. Alexandria, Va: Association for Supervision and Curriculum Development, 1984.

132. Stallings, Jane A. "Using Time Effectively: A Self-Analytic Approach." In *Improving Teaching,* edited by Karen K. Zumwalt. Alexandria, Va.: Association for Supervision and Curriculum Development, 1986.

133. Steinbrink, J. E. "The Social Studies Learner as Questioner." *Social Studies* 76, no. 1 (January/February 1985): 38–40.

134. Strong, Richard. "Teaching Styles and Strategies." Paper presented at National Curriculum Study Institute, sponsored by the Association for Supervision and Curriculum Development, Williamsburg, Va., August 1986.

135. Suydam, Marilyn N. "Low Achievers." *Arithmetic Teacher* 31, no. 4 (December 1983): 40.

136. Swick, Kevin J. *Disruptive Student Behavior in the Classroom.* 2d ed. Washington, D.C.: National Education Association, 1987.

137. Swick, Kevin J., and Hanley, Patricia E. *Stress and the Classroom Teacher.* Washington, D.C.: National Education Association, 1985.

138. Tobin, Kenneth. "Effects of Teacher Wait-Time on Discourse Characteristics in Math and Language Arts Classrooms." *American Educational Research Journal* 23, no. 2 (Summer 1986): 191–200.

139. Tolman, Marvin N., and Allred, Ruel A. *The Computer and Education.* Washington, D.C.: National Education Association, 1987.

140. Turnbaugh, Anne. "Urban High Schools Improving, but Many Problems Remain." *School of Education Newsletter,* University of Wisconsin-Madison, October 1986.

141. Tyler, Ralph W. "Using Research to Improve Teaching Effectiveness." In *Perspectives on Effective Teaching and the Cooperative Classroom,* edited by Judy Reinhartz. Washington, D.C.: National Education Association, 1984.

142. U.S. Department of Education. *Dealing with Dropouts: The Urban Superintendents' Call to Action.* Washington, D.C.: U.S. Government Printing Office, 1987.

143. _____. *What Works: Research About Teaching and Learning,* Washington, D.C.: U.S. Government Printing Office, 1986.

144. _____. *What Works. Schools That Work: Educating Disadvantaged Children.* Washington, D.C.: U.S. Government Printing Office, 1987.

145. Vance, James H. "The Low Achiever in Mathematics: Readings from the Arithmetic Teacher." *Arithmetic Teacher* 33, no. 5 (January 1986): 20–23.

146. Vitale, Barbara M. *Unicorns Are Real.* Rolling Hills Estates, Calif.: Jalmar Press, 1985.

147. Vobejda, Barbara. "A Generation at Risk." *Washington Post National Weekly Edition* (October 26, 1987): 6–8.

148. Walberg, Herbert. "Families as Partners in Educational Productivity." *Phi Delta Kappan* 65, no. 6 (February 1984): 397–400.

149. Wang, Margaret C., and Walberg, Herbert J., eds. *Adapting Instruction to Individual Differences.* Berkeley, Calif.: McCutchan, 1985.

150. Wehlage, Gary G.; Rutter, Robert A.; and Turnbaugh, Anne. "A Program Model for At-Risk High School Students." *Educational Leadership* 44, no. 6 (March 1987): 70–73.

151. Welsh, Patrick. *Tales Out of School.* New York: Elisabeth Sifton Books, Viking, 1986.

152. Wilen, William W. *Questioning Skills, for Teachers* 2d ed. Washington, D.C.: National Education Association, 1987.

153. Wilen, William W., ed. *Questions, Questioning Techniques, and Effective Teaching.* Washington, D.C.: National Education Association, 1987.

154. Wiles, Jon W., and Bondi, Joseph C. *Making Middle Schools Work.* Alexandria, Va.: Association for Supervision and Curriculum Development, 1986.

155. Williams, Patricia A.; Haertel, Edward H.; Haertel, Geneva D.; Walberg, Herbert J. "The Impact of Leisure-Time Television on School Learning: A Research Synthesis." *American Educational Research Journal* 19, no. 1 (Spring 1982): 19–50.

156. Wilson, John H. *The Invitational Elementary Classroom.* Springfield, Ill.: Charles C. Thomas, 1986.

157. Wiseman, Douglas E.; Hartwell, L. Kay; and Curlett, James. "Teaching the Low Achiever." *National Association of Secondary School Principals Bulletin* 64, no. 440 (December 1980): 92–100.

158. Wlodkowski, Raymond J. *Motivation.* Rev. ed. Washington, D.C.: National Education Association, 1986.

159. _____. *Motivation and Teaching: A Practical Guide.* Washington, D.C.: National Education Association, 1986.

160. _____. *The M.O.S.T. Program: Motivational Opportunities for Successful Teaching.* Phoenix, Ariz.: Universal Dimensions, 1983.

161. Yager, Stuart; Johnson, David W.; and Johnson, Roger T. "Oral Discussion, Group-to-Individual Transfer, and Achievement in Cooperative Learning Groups." *Journal of Educational Psychology* 77, no. 1 (February 1985): 60-66.

162. Young, M., ed. *Knowledge and Control.* London: Collier Macmillan Publishers, 1971.

OPERATION RESCUE

Each year more than one million children and young adults drop out of schools or are chronically truant. The consequences of dropping out, for both our nation and the individuals involved, are staggering. Dropouts are more likely to be unemployed than their graduate counterparts. When they are employed, dropouts earn approximately one-third less. Dropouts are more likely to be the parents of the next generation's underclass, and they tend to be overrepresented in our nation's prisons. The impact of dropping out on the lives of these children and on the future of our nation requires immediate, direct, and focused action.

Operation Rescue was created as a vehicle for initiating this action. In 1985, 1.7 million education professionals who are members of the National Education Association voted to contribute their own money to the National Foundation for the Improvement of Education (NFIE) to launch a national assault on the dropout crisis. For the first two years, $700,000 was designated for dropout prevention grants and for years to come, $1 million was earmarked to begin NFIE's endowment to make educational excellence grants available to teachers.

Operation Rescue is a multifaceted program. It centers on a strategy aimed at direct action and practical solutions. It includes grant giving, information exchanges, publications, and dissemination of results.

By continuing to build on the momentum that Operation Rescue has established, NFIE will further advance the empowerment of teachers, the restructuring of schools to improve education for all students, and the opportunity for each student to realize his or her full potential. This will enable students to have the knowledge, skills, and confidence to meet the challenges that they will face, and those that society will face in the future.

For further information contact:

THE NATIONAL FOUNDATION
FOR THE IMPROVEMENT OF EDUCATION
1201 16th Street, NW, Washington DC 20036 (202) 822-7840